Wise WOMEN Bearing GIFTS

Wise WOMEN Bearing GIFTS

Joys and Struggles of Their Faith

SUZAN D. JOHNSON, EDITOR

Judson Press ® Valley Forge

WISE WOMEN BEARING GIFTS

We are grateful to the following publications for permission to reprint their
material:
    "Alice Louise Wood Richards" by Tai Shigaki and "Marta Ezquilín" by Yamina
Apolinaris originally appeared in the Jan./Feb. 1987 issue of WATCHword,
a publication of the Women and the Church (WATCH) program of National
Ministries, American Baptist Churches in the U.S.A.

    "Carrie Bell Brown" by Kristy Arnesen Pullen and "Petra A. Urbina" by
Ronald J. Arena originally appeared in the July/August 1987 issue of
The American Baptist, a magazine published by the American Baptist Board
of Education and Publication.

Bible quotations in this volume are from:
    The Holy Bible, King James Version

    The Revised Standard Version of the Bible, copyrighted 1946, 1952, ©
1971, 1973 by the Division of Christian Education of the National Council
of the Churches of Christ in the U.S.A., and used by permission.

LIBRARY OF CONGRESS
Library of Congress Cataloging-in-Publication Data

    Wise women bearing gifts / edited by Suzan D. Johnson.
         p.   cm.
      ISBN 0-8170-1140-4 : $6.95
         1. Women clergy—United States—Biography.   2. Women Clergy—
      Puerto Rico—Biography.   I. Johnson, Suzan D.
      BR569.W57   1988
      277.3'082'0922—dc19   88-13032
      [B]   CIP

Dedicated to my parents,
Dorothy and Wilbert,
wise persons who affirmed
my humanity
while celebrating what divinity
was doing with my femininity.

Contents

Foreword

———✤———

S uzan D. Johnson has collected the life testimonies and descriptions of veteran women ministers—clergy and lay—in various stages and phases of their development, and in a marvelous variety of Christian service. Included are voices seldom, if indeed ever, heard by the vast majority of Christians. Their message, for the most part, bespeaks a quiet and often awesome endurance, in quest of the simple privilege of performing the selfless vocations to which they are sure God has called them.

At times poignant and deeply moving, these accounts remind us of the still unfinished business of the church's grave injustices to women. Seldom if ever do the subjects engage in hostile criticism, but the patient persistence of these women generates both profound respect and righteous indignation. *Nobody* should have to struggle so hard just to be given the right to be a blessing. God has been trying to break through for a long time.

Each personality is different, and each story is unique. The settings vary widely, and the needs found there sweep a wide gamut of the human condition. In every case, a courageous and compassionate saint responds in her own inimitable manner, despite a huge range of handicaps. One is prone to wonder what many male pastors would do when faced with similar hardships and extraministerial burdens. As one of the subjects suggests, God really needed the "womanpower" called, because their natural gifts and sensitivities are so appropriate to the multifaceted tasks of caring ministry.

This work is hard to lay down. Without rancor it simply allows the lives of dedicated and productive women to speak. "Sujay" Johnson has done the cause and her readership a great service.

Ella P. Mitchell
Atlanta

Introduction

*". . . Now when Jesus was born. . . . behold there came wise (wo)men
. . . and when they had opened their treasures, they presented unto him
gifts. . . ."   Mt. 2:1 & 11 (KJV)*

For seven of my thirty-one years I have been a gospel
preacher, one who felt and responded to the call of God.
Five of these years have been in the pastoral ministry at a
blessed place called Mariners' Temple Baptist Church, the oldest Baptist church on the island of Manhattan. As I received the
call to come there as interim pastor, most of my colleagues,
peers and critics felt this was truly a wilderness experience.
"How," they asked, "could you end up in Chinatown? Out of all
the Baptist churches in New York, why did you have to go so
far downtown?" Mariners' is at the lowest end of Manhattan, in
an area not known as residential but rather as a business community, and not known for having any black population at all.

The Asian presence and complexion of this geographic area
seemed to be a totally antithetical reality to a black female

Note: In some editorial styles the word "black" is capitalized. Judson Press follows
the policy that lowercases both "black" and "white" as they refer to persons.

pastor: For me there was really no choice. I'd learned that our difficulties become God's opportunities. Also, I learned early in life, both from experience and by sitting at the feet of those I consider wise, never to waste time or energy on those who do not share your dreams and visions. In the vernacular, "Don't hang with people who aren't headed where you are." I was excited. Any experience in ministry was a blessing to me.

I came to Mariners' the last semester of my senior year of seminary, while working in the denominational office and madly trying to meet my thesis deadline. (It was at Union Theological Seminary that I met four outstanding black professors whom I thank for affirming my gifts.) Prior to my call to Mariners', I had been in the ministry for three years, having had very few role models who were female and even fewer men who were willing to risk supporting women in ministry. I recalled a great-aunt Augusta who died shortly after I started grade school. She had wanted to be a "preacher" but was denied access to any pulpits. In fact, she had to travel to a "storefront church" in Baltimore just to be ordained.

As the hand of God so intricately weaves the tapestry of our lives, my brother and I were sent South for the summers as children to learn values from our maternal grandparents and to get off the streets of New York City. It was in a remote southern town, Concord, North Carolina, that I met my first role model, Katie G. Cannon, who later became the first black woman to be ordained in the Presbyterian Church. I was about thirteen at the time she was ordained and found a new door opened that I had never envisioned. Life would later find me pursuing all kinds of new adventures, performing on stage and screen and then landing a lucrative and successful career in television production. By the age of twenty-three I was earning more money than many people much older, yet there was still a small voice within telling me that I needed to do more with my life.

The insatiable desire to preach the gospel became unavoidably evident, so at twenty-three I publicly announced my call to the Christian ministry. Thanks be to God I was blessed to serve under a very open and honest pastor, Ollie Wells, who shared with me the joys and struggles of parish ministry and who dared to "show me the ropes." Ordination preparation led me to the American Baptist Churches of Metropolitan New York (ABC-Metro). It was this relationship that would ultimately change my life forever. Within one year exactly from my ordination date, I was called to serve my present charge. ABC-Metro was instrumental in opening an avenue.

The church had only fifteen members my first Sunday, worshipping in a sanctuary that holds more than one thousand. Many said that I was there for the final benediction. It was not considered by the "old boys' network" to be a "major" pulpit. In fact, most "serious" preachers did not even consider candidating for it. But there was one who was mightier than I who made the rough place smooth and this valley of despair into a mountain of hope, where now more than 550 of us are in community together, and another 500 businesspersons come to a weekly business service.

It was only, though, as we continued to experience this rapid growth, that I realized there was a distinct difference in being a female who expressed gifts for the ministry and one who was male who expressed the same desire. It thrust me into a new role for which I was not prepared—the role of pioneer, spokesperson, role model for women in ministry (all terms used by others in describing me). I found dozens of frustrated women ministers, many of whom were rejected in their home situations or frustrated to the point of quitting, visiting my church on Sundays or calling me at home. Their pain, in most cases, caused me to realize that we were called "for such a time as this" (Esther 4:14, RSV).

Being part of ABC-Metro Women in Ministry, which alone has more than seventy-five women, sometimes blinds me to situations outside of the metropolitan area. It was only as I began to receive national and international invitations as a result of the work at Mariners' that I realized that many, and I would venture to say most, women ministers' stories are quite different. Many have denied their calls, been blocked from exercising their gifts, or have spent so much time and energy crying about their plights that little or no energy is left to do the ministries to which they've been called. Hence, the need to minister to sisters *and* brothers across the continent became evident. Sisters who desire to bring their gifts to Jesus must be allowed their God-given rights and opportunities. The stories shared in this volume are the joys and struggles of sisters of faith, both in lay and ordained ministries, as seen by those who've admired and/or worked with them.

As I began to read the stories, I realized the pain and frustration I've suppressed in these past years from my Baptist brothers who will call me to march with them against injustice yet still refuse to admit women into their Monday conference or their pulpits; a male pastor who refused to baptize in the same water that I'd been in; the times I've received invitations because I am "a woman" and not because I am a preacher/pastor; the fellow pastor who asked me to marry him but later succumbed to peer pressure placed on him for being with a "woman preacher." Yet, I also recalled the great joys and rewards of seeing four students go away to college for the first time in each family's history; of seeing a high percentage of men return to the church; of baptizing more than 400 new converts to the Lord.

It is my prayer and hope that as New Testament Christians we remember the "surprise at sunrise" on that Easter morning when Christ was not in the tomb, confined, but risen for *all* of us. Christ rose that we, too, could be set free and use our treasures and gifts for his glory.

May you find joy and struggle in the pages that follow.

Suzan D. Johnson
Senior Pastor
Mariners' Temple Baptist Church
New York City

Sarah Small

by Regine Harding

*E*very morning at around 5 A.M., long before the winter sun has brought morning light into the streets of Roxbury, Massachusetts, Sarah Small gets up in her grand old second-floor Victorian bedroom at 41 Winthrop Street. By 5:30 she is already on the telephone with her brother in Baltimore to pray with him. Then she calls her many other prayer partners.

By 7:30 she is ready to catch a ride into Boston with her son, a legal services lawyer, to get to work. Sarah Small is the senior Protestant campus minister at the University of Massachusetts. Morning prayer on campus starts at 8:30 A.M. Prayer is the daily bread that has sustained her along the amazing road of her life's journey. "Whatever comes, pray about it," she believes. People used to say it was prayer and cigarettes that kept Mrs. Small going, but ten years ago the doctors threatened her into giving up smoking, so now it is mostly prayer.

Sarah Small's journey began in rural eastern North Carolina

where she grew up. The Baptist church was the way of life for her parents and grandparents. Sarah began early to assert some independence and had her own ideas about church. When she was asked to play the piano in other churches, she agreed, "providing you don't tell me how to live." This rebellious spirit that refused to be pushed into any mold is still with her. She insists on being who she is and no one else, especially not who other people expect her to be.

In these early years music kept her in the church and fed her faith. Although she was serious about church, she did not plan her life around it. Now as she looks back to this time she recalls, "The Lord had different things in mind for me."

Modest were the expectations for a young girl like Sarah growing up in the 1930s and 1940s in Williamston, North Carolina. Sarah could anticipate a few years of grammar school, some high school, perhaps a job in the cafeteria of the Negro school, marriage at an early age, a family of four or five children, years of struggle trying to make ends meet, and not much hope for change.

She was not sure what she wanted for her life. Yet by 1949 she was married and life was not easy. During this time she realized that in prayer she could hold on to some independence and a sense of who she really was to be, as she longed to break out of the expected pattern of life.

When the fire of the civil rights movement burned across the South, she was ready to respond, although it caught her by surprise. One day in 1963, Mr. Golden Frinks, the dapper community organizer of the Southern Christian Leadership Conference (SCLC), came to Williamston and explained about the freedom movement and how God was troubling the waters. Sarah Small came home one night and found a message written on a brown paper bag to come to a meeting at church that night. She was working with the young people in town and decided to get them to the meeting. She went back home, but then realized, "I'd better go and see what these men are telling the children . . . . They were getting ready to march! Believe me, I thought it was too early, too drastic."

Yet within a few days, Sarah Small, at thirty-six years of age, found herself in the center of the civil rights movement, and to her surprise "and the dismay of many" she was elected president of the Williamston Unit of the Southern Christian Leadership Conference. "I certainly had not planned for that," muses Sarah. "It was all God's will."

Along with thousands of others across the South, mostly children following the lead of Dr. King and others, she responded to the new spirit. Now she found that she could draw on what she had learned in church during those many years spent playing the piano. The hymns were meaningful.

> We've come this far by faith, Leaning
> on the Lord;
> Trusting in His Holy Word, He's never
> failed us yet.
> Oh, we can't turn back; We've come this
> far by faith.*

Change did not come easily to Williamston. For sixty consecutive nights in the summer of 1963, the children and a few adults of Williamston met for mass meetings in the Green Memorial Church. There was prayer, Scripture and preaching, and lots of singing with President Sarah Small at the piano. Every night after the mass meeting the group would march singing up to the City Hall to demonstrate. Every night the demonstrators, including several of Sarah's own children, were met with sticks. Blood was shed.

It was all so new. She was not prepared for this—practicing nonviolent civil disobedience, going to jail.

She started to speak in other communities, now really trusting in God. "Because when you are out of town, and you have no place to turn, there is nobody to rely on but God."

The civil rights movement was spreading across the face of the whole nation, and a group of white clergy from Boston felt that spirit. They called Dr. King one day and asked where they could go to join in the freedom movement, and the answer came:

*"We've Come This Far By Faith" by Albert A. Goodson, © 1963 by Manna Music, Inc., 25510 Ave. Stanford, Suite 101, Valencia, CA 91355. International Copyright Secured. All Rights Reserved. Used by Permission.

"Williamston, it's a dangerous city, but they could use your help."*

Early in October 1963, fifteen white clergymen drove to Williamston. After the first night at the mass meeting led by Mrs. Sarah Small, they humbly realized what a powerful leader she was. For them that first night at the Green Memorial Church remains unforgettable—the singing, the preaching, and Mrs. Small's simple, inspired message, "There's an old song which my mother taught me, which I've just recalled. 'All my heart this night rejoices.' " On she went simply giving her testimony of how the Lord had brought her out of bondage.

Here were fifteen seminary professors, denominational executives, church and community leaders from New England, sitting at the feet of this humble woman and saying, "Never has the gospel meant so much to me as it does when Mrs. Small teaches and lives it."

In the next year hundreds of northerners found their way to Williamston and to the Green Memorial Church. Sarah was invited North, once with her Freedom Choir of eighty children to hold a series of mass meetings around New England.

It seemed inevitable that eventually she would settle in Boston. In 1970 Sarah Small accepted an invitation to move to Packard Manse in Roxbury, an ecumenical community action center that owns the big old Victorian house that is still her home and where she continues her ministry.

Over the succeeding years that she has been in Boston, Sarah Small has touched many lives and inspired many people. Under her direction the house has become an important community center in Roxbury—a place to distribute supplemental food to hungry families and a refuge for homeless children and young people in transition, many of whom still keep in touch.

When the Boston Jewish community sought an emissary to visit Israel in 1972 to help work on greater understanding between divided people, they chose Mrs. Small. When the peace

*Paul K. Chapman, director of Packard Manse, an ecumenical conference center in Stoughton and Roxbury, Mass., during the years 1957 to 1975 who led the group to Williamston, gives this account from his friendship with Mrs. Small during these years.

movement sent a delegation to Paris to talk peace with the leaders of North Vietnam, Mrs. Small was chosen.

Today all this seems to be just preparation for what God still had in mind for Sarah Small. It was 1975 and times were hard; there was no money. Sarah prayed to God for an answer, as God had provided each time when life had been on the edge, and there had been nowhere to turn but prayer.

Meanwhile the Boston-Cambridge Ministries in Higher Education was looking for a Protestant campus minister for the University of Massachusetts.

One day Sarah received a letter in the mail about a job working with young people. She admits afterward she didn't really read the letter carefully and if she had she probably would not have applied. All she saw was something about teaching children about the Lord. And she did need a job.

She said to her son, "John, write me a resumé and tell the truth." The truth was that she had "not finished anything." She had no formal education. However, she had been to Israel and she had been to Paris, and she had worked with Dr. Martin Luther King, Jr., which she thinks carried a little weight. It must have, because after several interviews she was chosen to be the campus minister. Only then did it fully dawn on her that she would be a college chaplain when she had not ever been to college. Should she go back and say no? She really needed the money.

Sarah was scared. "When I received the call, I sat right here and prayed. The Lord gave me the 43rd chapter of Isaiah and said, 'I know you, I have called you by name. Just sit there and I'll teach you and tell you what to do.' "

Sarah Small learned by doing. For a while she could not figure out God's leading, and was waiting to hear that it was all a mistake. She still marvels at God's ways.

How unlikely in a world of credentials and academic degrees and titles that this woman from the rural South who didn't finish high school should be appointed senior minister and dean of the chapel in a prestigious Boston academic institution. At graduation it is she who marches down with all the "big shots" wearing fancy robes. It is she who gives the invocation.

Sarah Small chuckles at God's sense of humor, shaking her head. "Here I am, going over to Harvard once a week, having breakfast at the Faculty Club, and I say, 'Lord, I really don't know what to think about you—it's really funny.' "

Does she really belong there? Yes. She is very clear about that. Once on the job she realized that she had the qualifications—her life experience, her sense of self, her faith, and prayer! What life and prayer have taught her made her who she is.

What she has to offer she often finds missing in the academic system. She is critical of an education that does not teach children how to think for themselves, to use common sense, to search for the truth from their own experience. Today students look for answers they can just repeat. In her Bible study and debates with students, Sarah Small does not give ready-made answers, but rather teaches them to find their own answers and not be afraid to go against conventional norms.

"Sometimes I stand up and say, 'Look at me, I am nobody. God will work with me and work with you. God will not be partial toward only certain persons.' And this gives people hope. You speak when the Spirit tells you to speak."

Sarah is aware that in her assignment as campus minister she must not pretend to be someone she isn't. "I'll just be me," she says. Hierarchies and sacred cows do not intimidate Sarah Small. She does not hesitate to stop the chancellor of the university in the hall, put her arm on his shoulder, and pray with him because he needs it.

Several times Sarah has considered getting a degree or getting ordained, but each time she seems to get blocked. "God likes to work with some people in the raw."

"I'll just be me." It sounds so simple, yet it does not happen without breaking out of conventions, breaking down barriers, and knowing that it is God's will to set you free.

"I'll just be me" does not happen as long as women look for men's approval, says Sarah Small. "God can use anybody if God wants to use you and you are available. The Lord is not looking for ability but availability. You've got to be there when God is ready to use you." She laughs. "It's exciting! I enjoy it."

It is getting dark in the large living room at Packard Manse. The front door has been busy. Sarah's back has been hurting, probably from washing the stairs. The prayer meeting starts soon at six o'clock. "It's prayer that keeps me going."

Regine Harding is an ordained American Baptist minister living in New York. She received her M.Div. degree from Union Theological Seminary, New York, in 1984. Prior to entering the ministry, Ms. Harding studied and taught literature and philology and worked in the art business in New York. She immigrated from Germany in 1962.

Marilú Dones de Reyes

By Angel Luis Gutiérrez

*I*t was the year 1971. The Baptist Church of Ciénaga Alta, located in the mountains on the northeastern part of the island of Puerto Rico and close to the Yunque Rainforest, had been dying a slow but sure death under the leadership of a father and son pastoral team. For a long time that community of believers was playing the game of being alive, but it was only a step away from a spiritual grave. The pastoral team could not carry the work any further, and they were considering closing the doors of the building.

At the same time there was a woman who was on fire with evangelism as a member of the Canóvanas Baptist Church. Marilú Dones de Reyes was married and had three daughters. Her husband was a very active lay member of the same church. She had been a leader all her life. She had graduated from the University of Puerto Rico with top honors, and through her school days she had presided over all her classes. She had done graduate work in school administration and was the principal of an elementary-junior public school. She was considering an offer to become school superintendent for one of the school districts of Puerto Rico.

A Baptist denomination in that country was trying to break loose from old ways of interpreting the Bible and was looking for new ways to be faithful to the gospel. Their new executive secretary thought that being Baptist meant faithfulness to Christ and the Bible and a willingness to be a trailblazer under the guidance of the Spirit. He believed that in a community of believers gifts are not restricted to certain kinds of people and that God was calling some *women* to respond to the possibilities of the pastorate.

One of those women was Marilú Dones de Reyes, who believed at that time, and still does, that God is a living God who is interested in leading men and women to a life of service in the kingdom. God has different ways to let people know about the divine will for their lives. The executive secretary approached Mrs. Reyes about the possibility of the ministry as a new option in her Christian life. She laughed with her contagious laughter but answered that there were no women in the pastorate and that she was not worthy of that responsibility. She was asked by him to pray and think. Two members of the country church of Ciénaga Alta came to ask her to become their pastor. It was the second signal from the Lord.

"Early in the morning of the next day," she says, "the Lord spoke to me again, and I was sure that it was the will of the Lord. Although I did not like it, I obeyed. After being in the pastorate for six consecutive months, God brought many different people with the same message of confirmation: 'I called you to the pastorate.' God's self-revelation continued until I said, 'All right, Lord.' "

Marilú's husband was a great help and support in the process of making the decision and during her ministry. When she was very unsure about taking the church, he almost pushed her into it. He was sure that the Lord was calling her and every day insisted that she should accept the pastorate. She says, "I remember that once I was down and tired and sitting in a corner.

I was very sad, but I did not want to share it with anyone. Suddenly he came close to me and raised my hands. When I questioned him about his action, he said that he was doing what Aaron did for Moses. His commitment to the Lord; his understanding of my multiple responsibilities as wife, mother, and pastor; and his willingness to sacrifice have been an inspiration to my life." He later became her associate pastor, and now they have a team ministry, and better than that—a family ministry. Their oldest daughter is a graduate of the School of Law of the University of Puerto Rico but works as youth pastor in the church, and her husband is in charge of the pastoral department. Dagmar, their second daughter, is a counselor at the church's day school, and her husband is also a teacher in that school. The youngest daughter is in the university and planning to be a missionary doctor.

It is interesting that the people who influenced the ministry of Marilú are all men—her husband; the executive secretary who recommended her to the church and who still keeps track of her; and the Rev. Dr. Félix Castro Rodríguez, the late pastor of First Baptist Church at Carolina, Puerto Rico.

Marilú Dones de Reyes is not only a woman pastor but one who does not fit any pattern. That means that she has been under fire from all sides. She was criticized by the "old guard" Baptist churches of Puerto Rico who thought her ministry was against the traditions of Baptists and the Bible. They were not willing to accept a woman pastor. She remembers the first time that she went to a pastors' retreat. A fellow pastor came to her and very bluntly said that he did not accept women pastors. She only smiled and told him to ask the Lord who had called her. When the speaker for the conference came in and said (without knowing anything about the previous conversation) that it would be a privilege for him to have Marilú as his pastor, she did not have to say another word in defense of her ministry during the whole retreat.

She is criticized by the Baptists and other mainline denominations for her charismatic approach to the worship and work of the church. At the same time, she is always under fire from the Pentecostal and other charismatic groups because she uses makeup and wears up-to-date fashions. She is always very careful about the way that she appears in public. During radio broadcasts, one Pentecostal pastor called her the Jezebel of the Baptists and a prostitute because of her use of makeup. She never defended herself of those criticisms. When the Pentecostal pastor met her for the first time, he confessed to her that he held her in high esteem.

Marilú says that all those experiences, negative and positive, have been blessings to her. They formed her character and strengthened her faith in the Lord. She has never been frustrated nor discouraged because she is sure of the One who called her. She has never been on the defensive nor felt inferior to any male pastor. "The Lord who called me has always defended me without my personal intervention," she says.

Pastor Marilú Dones de Reyes has beat her male colleagues at their own game since they always thought that a good pastor is characterized by a growing membership at the church, by the raising of the budget, and by the building of temples and huge organizations and institutions. Her credentials based on those characteristics surpass any other church on the island of Puerto Rico.

In her seventeen years as pastor, the congregation at Ciénaga Alta has grown from a handful of people to more than 2000 members, and it keeps growing. There were 565 baptisms in 1987, with an average of about 150 baptisms every three months. About 600 persons have been added to the roll during the past year. Sunday morning attendance averages 2000 persons, and about 3000 people attend special services on the last Sunday of every month. A weekly Wednesday morning service is usually attended by 300 persons and is broadcast to the whole island. Marilú has taken her enthusiasm to New York City; Bridgeport; Connecticut; and Florida, and also to places like the Dominican Republic, Costa Rica, Bolivia, and Venezuela. In those places and at nine other places on the island, the congregations have numbered up to 1220 persons.

She appears on two TV channels in Puerto Rico and also in New York, Connecticut, California, Chicago, Wisconsin, Costa Rica, and Venezuela. She has radio programs in different cities in Puerto Rico, in the United States, and in some Latin American countries.

Mrs. Reyes has not forgotten her responsibility to the community and has worked to improve it by trying to contribute to healing some of the problems. Her church has founded a day school from kindergarten to high school. It also has a day care center and another center to provide clothing, food, and furniture. In January 1988 a suicide prevention program was started with a telephone line that receives calls twenty-four hours a day. The church is acquiring sixty acres of land to develop programs for older citizens, orphans, and people with different physical, emotional and spiritual needs.

Marilú is a great communicator from the pulpit and also on a one-to-one basis, but she also uses the mass media. Besides preaching on television and radio, she uses daily newspapers, books, and a monthly magazine that is published by her church.

Her ministry has been characterized by practicing divine healing and helping people with personal and family problems.

Marilú Dones de Reyes was chosen by God to be a trailblazer for women in ministry in Puerto Rico, but God had more in mind—a woman who could show that God gives gifts to those who are willing to use them to the highest. She has been faithful to that, and God has blessed her ministry beyond what anyone expected seventeen years ago.

The Reverend Angel Luis Gutiérrez is associate professor of Christian Ministries and director of Hispanic Life at Eastern Baptist Theological Seminary in Philadelphia, Pa. Previously, he pastored several churches in Puerto Rico and served as executive secretary of the Puerto Rican Baptist Convention. Rev. Gutiérrez earned his bachelor's degree from Bluffton College in Ohio and the Master of Divinity degree from the Evangelical Seminary of Puerto Rico.

Andrea —
The gift of your
friendship, uncompromising
support has inspired me over
and over. God guide
through the pages of your
and give you faith!
Love, Elinor

R. Elinor Hare

by Barbara Eyvonne Headley

———❦———

T he letter and flier came across my desk, buried beneath a pile of unopened mail, in late September of 1985. As I perused the mail, the letterhead "Women's Advocate Ministry" caught my eye. The letter, written by a Rev. Elinor Hare, briefly described the ministry as support for women defendants who were incarcerated at the Women's House of Detention on Rikers Island, the largest jail in the New York City area.

I did not know in what way the organization offered support to the women defendants on Rikers, but I did know that at that time there were over 700 women (which had increased to over 1000 by 1987) held at Rikers Island. I was also painfully aware that 95 percent of these women were black and Hispanic, between the ages of 18 and 30, poor, uneducated, unskilled, and imprisoned mostly for economic crimes. Because I felt powerless in finding a meaningful way to help these incarcerated sisters, I was anxious to find out just what the Women's Advocate Ministry was all about.

The letter described the ministry as a volunteer advocacy program for women defendants in the courts and at Rikers Island Jail. It also announced a volunteer training session to be conducted by Rev. Elinor Hare for prospective volunteers and interested persons the following Saturday. I made plans to attend.

The meeting was held at the Lafayette Presbyterian Church in Brooklyn. I did not know what to expect. I did not know Rev. Hare. Being Baptist, I was not very familiar with my clergy sisters of other denominations. However, because of the nature of such a ministry, I did have some preconceived ideas about the kind of woman who would undertake such a task. All my preconceived notions were dismissed that morning when I met Elinor Hare for the first time.

She came unassumingly into the room, and except for the fact that she was wearing a clerical collar and had preceded to the front, I would not have thought her to be the organizer and primary advocate for incarcerated women in New York City. She was about five and a half feet tall with pale blue eyes, short gray hair, and a soft, gentle voice. She appeared to be in her middle fifties. She introduced herself as Rev. Elinor Hare, a minister of the United Methodist Church and the founder of the Women's Advocate Ministry in Courts and Jail. As I listened to her presentation, I wondered to myself, *Who is this gentle, subdued, older white woman, who dared to challenge the criminal justice system of New York City on the behalf of minority women with whom she probably had nothing in common except gender?* I knew that there was something very special about this woman.

Elinor grew up on a farm near Jamestown, New York, during the Depression. She was one of six children. Her four brothers and one sister were born with a hearing weakness which later developed into total hearing loss. Despite the handicaps, there was a great deal of sibling love. Her father died when she was five. At the age of seventeen, shortly after she had graduated from high school, Elinor suffered another loss. Her mother died suddenly of a cerebral hemorrhage. The early death of her parents shattered her dream to go to college. With few options open to her and with a sense of helplessness, she got married at the age of seventeen to a man she barely knew.

The marriage was a difficult and abusive one. She soon discovered that her husband was an alcoholic. After five years of abuse, she left him, taking their three small children with her. Along with a sense of relief, she also felt a sense of guilt and worthlessness because her marriage had failed. The early 1950s was a time when a woman's worth was measured by her marriage and domestic skills. She struggled to take care of her children and herself, but there were few opportunities for a woman who had no marketable skills. She had to be sustained by public assistance, a situation which further decreased her sense of self-worth. It was during this time that Elinor had an encounter with God, one that would change the course of her life.

When her children were invited by a neighbor to a Vacation Bible School at a local church, she refused to let them attend at first, having a distrust for the church. She had not had much of a religious upbringing herself, and the difficulties of her life led her to resent God and the church. But something drew her to the church that summer of 1955, something that spoke to her needs and to her heart, something that reached out to embrace and affirm her, not only as a child of God but as a woman of worth.

While attending a tent meeting, Elinor gave her life to Christ. Almost immediately her life was transformed from one of helplessness and poor self-esteem to one of faith, both faith in God and in herself. The church nurtured and supported her as she grew in Christ. It was during this time that she met Rosalind Lesher. Rosie was also a single parent, trying to raise two children who were about the same age as Elinor's children. Rosie, who had been a Christian since her childhood, helped Elinor understand and adjust to her new life as a Christian. They became close and dear friends. They shared not only their faith but also the responsibility of caring for and raising their children together.

The women decided to go into business together. Elinor, aware of her natural talent to fix hair, but without formal train-

ing, took the beauticians' licensing exam and passed. She and
Rosie then opened a beauty shop in their shared home. Elinor
was unable to acquire a bank loan because she was an unmarried
woman, so she borrowed the funds to get started from a woman
who was a member of their church. Elinor was the beautician;
Rosie the bookkeeper. They managed the shop together for
twenty years.

Elinor had also begun to study Scripture privately. She recognized that Scripture fed something deep within her, something
that thirsted for truth, justice, equality, and righteousness, particularly for women. Believing that with God all things were
possible, she began to dream again of going to college. She had
not thought of this possibility since her parents' death almost
twenty years before. Already in her forties, she thought that she
might be too old to attend college, but with encouragement from
friends and with her trust in God, she applied to the community
junior college in her town. While still operating the beauty shop
from her home, she began taking classes, completing her associate degree within two years. This began an insatiable desire for
knowledge. A whole new world was opening up for Elinor. She
was accepted at the State University of New York at Fredonia.
She commuted to classes, while still operating the beauty shop,
and completed her B.A. degree in sociology in only three and a
half years. During her last semester at Fredonia, she took a
course in religion. It was while taking this course that she
sensed her call to the ministry.

Her call to the ministry became clear within her soul as her
own spirit witnessed to the change in her life and in her desires,
but it was still a time of struggle and denial for her. Old fears
and the feelings of inadequacy returned. Elinor was now forty-
seven years old, a grandmother, and experiencing difficulties
with her health, having been diagnosed as a diabetic. She had
remained active in her local church. She was a Sunday school
teacher and a member of a group of Methodist women who
provided special programs on missions in local churches. While
these services were meaningful, she felt that they did not qualify
her for ministry.

She continued to argue with God, trying to escape her own

destiny. She did not know any women ministers personally, and those she had heard of were younger. Who would take seriously a middle-aged grandmother and beautician who felt that she had been called to the ministry? She felt intimidated by the prospect and ill-equipped for the task. But despite the feelings of inadequacy and fear of rejection, Elinor pursued her calling.

In 1972 she met with the District Board of Ordained Ministers to declare her call to ministry. She was the only woman present among several young men. When her time came to be interviewed, she entered the room and found the all-male board sitting behind a conference table. In the center of the room was the candidate's chair—a rocking chair. She did not know whether the other candidates had had to sit in the rocker, but it was evident that it was the only seat available to her. She recalled the feelings of intimidation and fear, but she took her seat and proceeded with her interview.

The meeting was informal. The board, while honoring the declaration of her call, tried to convince her not to bother with formal seminary training. They suggested that she pursue instead the more traditional course of study offered by the United Methodist Church for local pastors. This would qualify her to become a deacon, but not an elder. Elinor rejected this and was insistent that she would pursue formal seminary training.

When the interview was over, she was approached by one of the board members. "Elinor," he said, "it took a lot of courage to do what you did today, and I like that. I just want you to know that you have a friend. Don't give up." She expressed her appreciation of his support but knew in her heart that now that she had begun, she would never give up until she had accomplished God's will for her life.

In January of 1974, with their children grown and on their own, Elinor and Rosie moved to New York City so that Elinor could attend Union Theological Seminary and Rosie could accept a position with the United Methodist Church office. While attending seminary, Elinor was ordained as a deacon in 1975. In May of 1977 she received her Master of Divinity degree. It was a moment of triumph.

In 1978, when the time for her to be ordained as elder was

approaching, she was hospitalized with a severe respiratory condition. It was doubtful whether she would survive to be ordained. As she lay in the intensive care unit just days before she was to be ordained, she had a dream in which she was given the assurance of God that she would be healed. When she awoke, she knew within her spirit and within her body that she was healed. To her physician's surprise, she was quickly well enough to be released from the hospital. Two days later, physically weak but full of faith in God, she was ordained as an elder of the United Methodist Church.

She served for two years as the senior pastor of a small inner-city United Methodist church in Buffalo. This was a rewarding experience, but an experience in Chicago in 1976 was what shaped the future of her ministry.

While working at the Women's Division of the United Methodist Church office in the Interchurch Center in New York, Elinor was sent to Chicago to observe a prison ministry program sponsored by the Institute of Women Today, directed by Sister Margaret Ellen Traxler. It was here that Elinor met Sister Joellen Sbrissa, a nun who worked with the program. Sister Joellen provided dance and yoga instruction for female inmates at the Cook County Jail. Elinor observed the program and noticed another level of interaction between the female inmates and Sister Joellen. Many of the women were being counseled by the sister, and she was making arrangements to be present in court on the days of their trials. Sister Joellen explained that many of the women had no family members or friends who would be present during this difficult experience. Sister Joellen offered to be present in court to give them support and assist during the crisis time of conviction and sentencing. The next day Elinor went with Sister Joellen. What she observed changed her life and gave new meaning to her calling and her ministry.

The court scene was a chaotic and frightening experience. There was a never-ending presentation of cases, with private and public attorneys, many of whom barely knew their clients, trying to make deals and arranging for postponements and delays. It seemed to be the last place where justice could take place. The defendants were confused and alone, appearing only for a few moments before they were returned to the court pens and then back to jail. Many did not know who their attorneys were.

The pens served as a holding area for inmates coming in from the jails before appearing in court. When she entered them, Elinor was shocked at what she saw. Contained in a large cage were several women, handcuffed and huddled together. It was dark and cold with nowhere to sit. In one corner was an open toilet. Many of the women had been there for hours without anything to eat. Lying on the floor, uncovered, was a pregnant woman. The scene was shocking and unforgettable. It was then that the Holy Spirit spoke to her, and Elinor knew what she was called to do and whom she was called to serve.

When she returned to New York she knew in her heart what her ministry must be. But how would she get started? Where would she begin? There were no programs with access to the courts and court pens in the New York City jail system. She realized then that she would have to start one herself. She knew little about the criminal justice system, so in 1980 she began attending the John Jay College of Criminal Justice in New York City, where she received her Master of Criminal Justice degree in 1983.

Then she began volunteering with various organizations and programs involved in criminal justice. One such program was The Citizen Advocates for Justice, directed by Connie Baugh. Connie had twenty years experience with the system and taught Elinor a great deal. While volunteering and visiting the courts and jails, Elinor began to work towards organizing what was now her dream, a ministry of advocacy for women in court and in jail. She didn't know where to begin since nothing like this had ever been done before and there was great opposition from many people, particularly the system. With assistance she wrote several proposals for the envisioned ministry and sent them to friends, pastors, church officials, organizations, and criminal justice officials. She didn't know what to expect but trusted that God would open a door.

In 1983 the Council of Churches of New York agreed to sponsor the advocacy ministry if Elinor could first raise enough money to support the ministry for one year. Through hard work she was able to raise twenty thousand dollars to sustain the ministry for one year. It was then that the Women's Advocate Ministry in Courts and Jails came into existence.

In 1984 the Women's Advocate Ministry (WAM) was granted official approval by the Department of Corrections, with access to the jails, court rooms, and the court pens. Now incorporated, WAM has served over four hundred incarcerated women. For these women, incarceration has been a devastating and dehumanizing experience. Because they are women, they have often been treated with added scorn and contempt. WAM gives physical and spiritual support to these women when no one else will or can.

Working alone for three years, Elinor has brought compassion and mercy to an otherwise harsh and evil situation. Daily she goes to court and to the court pens, where she ministers to women who are broken in spirit and in body. She makes contact with inmates' families and attorneys and arranges for women to see and be with their children while in jail. Quiet and unassuming, Elinor's presence is felt and known in the courts and jails of New York City. She is affectionately known by the female inmates and the correctional officers as the "Blue Nun" because of her familiar blue suit and light blue clerical shirt.

In 1986, Elinor was accepted to the Doctor of Ministry program at Drew University in New Jersey. She completed her course work in 1987 and is presently working on her professional project, which involves the work she has done with the advocacy program.

Elinor's life is not one of glamour or fame. She, like many women, struggled to find her own identity and self-worth. Maybe this is why she can reach out so effectively to others. Although their background and life circumstances may be unlike her own, Elinor holds the bond of sisterhood. From an obscure farm in upstate New York, from an unlikely generation, and from an unexpected profession, Elinor was called by God to be subject to the Spirit and to embody God's justice.

I watch Elinor Hare as she ministers to women who have been rejected by society. I watch her gentleness and know that her own life has not been easy but that she has had faith in a God who could do the impossible. I watch her reach out in love and mercy to those who need to know that someone does care.

A young woman whose own life has been a nightmare of poverty and abuse is convicted of manslaughter and immediately sentenced to fifteen years to life in prison. When she is taken back to the court pens, there is a familiar figure waiting for her. No words are exchanged because no words can express the pain, sorrow, fear, and regret. Elinor Hare opens her arms to the trembling woman, embraces her, and allows her to cry uncontrollably. All that matters now is that this young woman knows that someone is there for her and that someone cares. In the cold, silent darkness of the court pens the words of Jesus can be heard: "I was naked and you clothed me, I was sick and you visited me, I was in prison and you came unto me."

The Reverend Barbara E. Headley is assistant/associate minister of Trinity Baptist Church in Bronx, New York, and dean of the Trinity Bible Institute. She worked professionally as a physical therapist before accepting her call to the Christian ministry in 1982. A Benjamin E. Mays Fellow for Ministry, she earned the Master of Divinity degree from Union Theological Seminary. She serves as an instructor of the Contemporary Ministries division of the National Baptist Congress of Christian Education. Rev. Headley serves on the board of directors of the Women's Advocate Ministry, Inc. and is currently a candidate for the Doctor of Ministry degree at Hartford Seminary, Hartford, Connecticut.

Ellen Tarry

by E. Terry Hamilton

W ith the eyes of a scholar and the smile of a well-loved child who is open to every experience and challenge, Ellen Tarry is living life fully and still passing on the faith. At eighty-one she has hands that look like they belong to a lady of leisure. But they are strong hands and with them she grabs hold of life. She grabs the good—her faith and her family—and the tough—she walked in Montgomery in 1965 with Dr. Martin Luther King, Jr. From the time of her childhood, her faith has caused her to work in the service of others. She has authored books for children and adults, among them: *Hesekiah Horton* (1942), *My Dog Rinty* (1946), *The Runaway Elephant* (1950), *Martin de Porres—The Saint of the New World* (1963), *Young Jim—The Early Years of James Weldon Johnson* (1967), and *The Other Torussaint* (1981). *My Dog Rinty* was a sensation. It portrayed a typical black family in Harlem. The book showed them as loving, caring, hard-working and organized, unlike the portrayal in most books written about Harlem and blacks of that day.

Ellen Tarry was born into a happy home in Birmingham, Alabama, in 1906, the daughter of a barber and a country girl who had settled in this coal and steel town. Her father, John Barber Tarry, called "Bob," was a mulatto and a Congregationalist. Her mother, Eula, was an octoroon, a person of one-eighth Negro ancestry. Eula Tarry was a beautiful woman with blue eyes and long red hair and an especially beautiful spirit that had been nurtured by the Methodist Church. Ellen's father was a man of religious principle and strong convictions. He tithed ten percent of his income to the church and raised funds among his white clients for the black churches of Birmingham. When she was young, her mother lovingly described Ellen as "a duke's mixture." She is rich in spirit and long on hard work.

Her childhood home was encircled by seven Protestant churches and people were always stopping by on their way to or from church services. Her father loved all types of music and took her to recitals. She remembers her mother singing the spirituals her father loved best: "Give Me That Old Time Religion," "Just Break the News to Mother," and "In the Baggage Coach Ahead." Ellen felt equally comfortable in all the churches closest to her home, but she loved Sixteenth Street Baptist best for its boys and Bible drills.

At these neighboring churches, someone was always lecturing about Africa or sending letters from missionaries to the Congregational church. Read aloud, the letters told of the Africans' hunger for Christ and their openness to the teachings of Jesus, as well as their need for education and food. Ellen visited the old folks' home, sold junk and gave the pennies she earned to the missionary fund. She "played" at being a preacher going off to work in Africa. As she grew, she vowed that she would become a missionary.

Through quirks of fate, her mother's familiarity with the Catholic Church and Ellen's friend's attendance at a convent school, Ellen went to St. Francis de Sales Institute, a high school for black girls, in Virginia. St. Francis, where Ellen converted to

Catholicism, was run by the Sisters of the Blessed Sacrament. Although it was a hard decision to convert, she firmly held that, "God will not be outdone. Everything will be all right." With her mother's blessing Ellen was eventually baptized on the Feast of the Immaculate Conception in December of 1922.

After completing her schooling, attending Alabama State, and beginning a teaching career in the South, Ellen eventually moved to New York City to study journalism at Columbia University. Those plans were not to be. The scholarship she needed fizzled out when the newspaper she worked for went bankrupt.

From the accepting, supportive and protective environment of her southern home and school, New York and especially Harlem were an immediate contrast. Working as a waitress and elevator operator, she felt isolated and lonely. She did not find a religious sister or priest mentor, as she had had in the South, until she met Father Michael F. Mulvoy. She recalls that he was referred to as, "the blackest white man in Harlem." He immediately put her to work with community people. One of her first tasks was to foster better race relations between blacks and whites. Omicron Omicron raised money to set up a race relations bureau on West 138th Street and got jobs for all blacks, not just Catholic blacks. Eventually this led Ellen to work with Father Mulvoy to get blacks jobs with the local utility company, the telephone company and the Fifth Avenue Bus Company at a time when few blacks worked or owned businesses in Harlem.

It was also during this period that Ellen began her association with Baroness Catherine de Hueck at Friendship House, a Catholic charity settlement house in Harlem. Later with a colleague, she opened and directed a Friendship House in Chicago at the request of Bishop Bernard J. Sheil. Tireless, Ellen worked for the March on Washington sponsored by A. Phillip Randolph which was planned for 1941 but was not held because of pressure brought action by F.D.R. Years later, in 1963, Ellen would march on Washington—this time with both A. Phillip Randolph and Dr. Martin Luther King, Jr.

Taught the worth of dignity and pride for black people in her home, she brought it as a value to her work. After visiting the City of St. Jude in Alabama, a self-help program for the poor, she wanted to institute a similar program orientation at Friendship House. This focus on increasing the participation and dignity of community people led to a painful strain in her relationships at Friendship House.

In the sparsely populated South, priests were few. They were more welcoming of help and leadership from laypeople in the work of the church. In New York City, priests resented the initiatives Ellen took in her work with the National Catholic Community Service-U.S.O. and assistance in ministry that she had grown used to offering.

As white Communists in Harlem were making inroads in wooing black men to their cause, Ellen was writing features for the *Amsterdam News,* a major black newspaper and for *America* and *Commonweal* magazines, two preeminent Catholic magazines, in addition to publishing books she authored. Ellen wrote of her experience with the Catholic church in an article in *Commonweal* called "Native Daughter." This was her response to Richard Wright's *Native Son.* She says, "just as the Communists had Richard Wright, the Catholic church had Ellen Tarry."

Ellen's life has not been easy. Through difficult times of a bad marriage and the birth of a daughter, whom she raised as a single parent, being mistaken for white and disliked because she was light-complexioned, she has kept to the faith of her mother and grandmother. She has lived a life of prayer as part of her everyday activities and lived a life of practical religion, doing for others as her grandparents and parents had done. Ellen Tarry demonstrates that "the seed of faith is never lost."*

*A wise saying of the black community.

E. Terry Hamilton is a black, Catholic feminist who is the vice-president of the National Assembly of Religious Women (a Catholic social justice ministry), a commissioner for the Office of Black

Ministry for the Archdiocese of New York and a former coordinator of the Woodstock-St. Paul Community. She holds a graduate degree from Columbia University; was named an Outstanding Young Woman in America in 1983; and has worked professionally as an executive and consultant in social services, women's spirituality and education.

Kim Mammedaty

by Janice M. Rounds

❦

K im Mammedaty, a Kiowa Indian, remembers the struggles and pain that alcohol has caused in many Indian families that she has known through the years.

Kim is the first seminary-trained Native American woman to be ordained by the American Baptist Churches, USA. She is now the pastor of the First American Baptist Church of Hobart, Oklahoma. The congregation is predominantly Indian and Kim is actively involved in organizing workshops on alcoholism for the church and community. Her vision is to expand this educational effort and to establish a halfway house in Hobart, specifically designed for Indian women recovering from the disease.

The youngest of ten children, Kim was born in Lawton, Oklahoma, and grew up a number of miles away in the western Oklahoma community of Mountain View. Kim says, "I do have good memories, especially of the stories my parents would tell,

Indian legends told at night. These stories told of how we evolved as a people. They have helped me realize that it is very important for me to remember my Indian heritage."

Though her large family was poor, there was a tremendous closeness, which is true of Indian people in general. "The extended family plays a very important part in Indian life," says Kim. Because of these close ties, according to Kim, the effects of alcohol are far-reaching. If an aunt, uncle or other relative suffers from the disease, the rest of the family is directly affected also. Kim remembers, "There was a lot of drinking in my family and with it, violence. I grew up with that reality."

To Kim, some of the basic issues of alcoholism today are the same regardless of race—issues such as trust, lack of communication and the numbness that all of the affected people feel.

Indian people have been particularly devastated by the introduction of alcohol into their society. States Kim, "It came at a time when Indian history was changing. Europeans were coming into America and just as they brought the grief of smallpox into Indian life, the introduction of alcohol was equally destructive to Indian people. It was used by whites to control and manipulate the Indians."

She continues, "Indian people had no role model for the prudent use of the substance and it soon became a source of escape from the pain of their changing world. For many Indian people their rituals and spiritual life—positive tools for handling stress and pain—were taken away by the non-Indians. Alcohol was now there to take the place of healthy ways of dealing with difficult issues."

Kim's family was no different. Alcohol played a significant role in the separation of Kim's parents. When she was eight years old the family broke apart. Kim, a brother and a sister were placed in the first of three foster homes. For five years during this very traumatic time, Kim was not allowed to see her parents. She recalls, "When I was thirteen, my parents reconciled. I managed to sneak away to visit them. They lived only one-half mile from the foster home. At fourteen I was permitted to visit them on holidays and at fifteen we were reunited. However, alcohol continued to be a problem."

The family remained together and Kim was encouraged by her parents to attend church. There, at the Rainy Mountain Kiowa Indian Baptist Church, near Anadarko, Oklahoma, she was nurtured by the congregation and by her pastor, Tom Lucas. It was he who first told her that someday she would be a minister.

Her thoughts about women in ministry first were sparked by Ioleta McElhaney, a Kiowa woman who came to the church to preach. She impressed Kim because she was an Indian woman who told interesting stories and preached the gospel.

In college, Kim began to become serious about her faith. At Eastern College in St. Davids, Pennsylvania, Kim observed students and professors who lived their faith. She says, "I began to realize that God is a liberator. God liberated us from bondage. Up to that point I never believed I could make it through college. The experience was overwhelming to me. But I received encouragement. I saw that as a sign of God working. Deuteronomy 31:8 became very important to me: 'It is the Lord who goes before you; he will be with you, he will not fail you or forsake you; do not fear or be dismayed'" (RSV).

Many at Eastern College were actively involved in fighting oppression and injustice, specifically United States policies regarding El Salvador. "The God I came to know during those years was a God who loved poor and oppressed people. That was me and how I felt about our people," she says. "I felt called to the oppressed, people who are left out."

The experiences at college were an important part of the faith journey of this young Kiowa woman. Kim remembers, "It changed my faith, my image of God. God loved the oppressed! God wanted the body of Christ to be involved in issues of justice. That was life-changing for me!"

Kim now realized she wanted to be involved in ministry so that she could empower her own people. "A new image of God was revealed to me. That was tremendously good news. God didn't want Indian people to be oppressed." Kim's plans for the ministry took on definite direction one summer while working on the Navajo Indian Reservation at Keams Canyon, Arizona. She decided to go to seminary.

Upon graduation from Eastern College, Kim enrolled at Colgate Rochester Divinity School.* During that time, she worked at the Tuscarora Mission on the Tuscarora Indian Reservation near Niagara Falls, New York.

Kim was ordained in 1985 at her home church. She served as pastor of the Bacone College Baptist Church in Muskogee, Oklahoma, before coming to the church she now serves in Hobart.

In her work at the Tuscarora Mission, Keams Canyon, and Bacone College and through her own life experience, Kim has also had to deal with another issue—racism.

She explains, "I've known from the age of five that I was different. As one of only three or four Indians in the public school, I remember comments from the non-Indian children. Those children in my kindergarten class made fun of me because of the color of my skin and my poor clothing. Because of the comments of non-Indians I have always felt my accomplishments were not as good as others'. I'm a 'good' Indian to them. Comments such as 'That's really good for an Indian' were hurtful. One woman in seminary implied my presence there was due to 'filling a quota' rather than because of my abilities."

The comments still continue, but attitudes are changing. Indian people are becoming leaders and this is how non-Indian people's attitudes can be changed. "Indian people have so much to offer this world," says Kim. "Indian people can bring a different perspective to a variety of issues."

Because of the experiences of racism and the memories and observations of what alcohol can do to a family and a people, Kim's ministry today deals with both issues. However, she firmly believes that beating the problem of alcohol is paramount to the improvement of all aspects of the lives of Indian people.

*Colgate Rochester Divinity School/Bexley Hall/Crozer Theological Seminary

Her vision of a halfway house specifically for Indian women meets a pressing need. There is only one facility in the state designed just for Indian women. Kim explains, "This lack of services for Indian women is a major concern. Women in most treatment centers usually remain there for twenty-eight to thirty days. They often have to return home to see others in their family continuing to drink. This is an environment that is not supportive to a recovering alcoholic."

The Hobart halfway house would enable women to learn to live on their own. Their stay would be flexible, but averaging three to six months. They would be encouraged to find employment, obtain their GED (General Equivalency Diploma) and thus gain self-confidence. The halfway house itself could be a source of employment for women who are successfully recovering. These women could serve as positive role models for others.

Kim Mammedaty is working hard to raise the interest and funds needed to open such a place. She is convinced that the church should play a major role in solving the problem of alcohol. "We (the church) must show Indian people that God is a loving God. The church should be a welcoming body of faith, not a judgmental community. The church must be the starting point. The entire Indian community needs to be involved in recovery. Indians are a community-oriented people. That is why the church is so important. Alcohol destroys Indian communities. The church needs to be a healing family for those suffering."

Kim ministers in her church and community to show her people a loving and forgiving God, a God who understands pain and grief and waits to embrace hurting people with love and hope.

"Everywhere I go, I am encouraged and empowered by other Indian people who are keeping the faith and moving forward. I receive such a blessing when I see our people growing. There is hope in recovery from alcoholism," says Kim.

Through her love and commitment to her people, Kim Mammedaty is one of those who empowers others to have the quality of life that is meant for all of God's children.

Janice M. Rounds is a free-lance writer and educator living in Southern California. She was the manager of mission interpretation for National Ministries, American Baptist Churches, USA from 1985–87.

Alice Louise Wood Richards

by Tai Shigaki

To many students at Denison University during the 1940s and 1950s, Alice Richards was known as "Mommie R." To me she was truly a mother substitute the forty-three years we were able to share our time and thoughts together.

My first encounter with Alice Richards was on a dreary Sunday morning in January of 1943. I had spent the night on a Greyhound bus arriving from the Rohwer relocation camp in Arkansas where I had been with my sister who was still confined there. At 1:00 A.M. I was let off at the bus stop in front of the local drugstore in the village of Granville. How arrangements got made in the middle of a Saturday night when there wasn't a soul around I don't know. But the next thing I knew I was comfortably ensconced in the lounge of one of the college dormitories on the hill. It was there that Mommie R. found me. She took me home and immediately set about making me feel at home and a part of the family. We went to the Granville Baptist

Church where I was introduced as her "other daughter." That very night their only daughter, Margie, was to be "pinned" via telephone to a Dartmouth man. This was all a surprise to Margie but her parents were part of the plot. This was a very special day in their lives and I arrived at what seemed such an inopportune time. But I would never have guessed it the way I was welcomed and made to feel right at home. Even in the excitement of the pinning I was included as though I had been a part of the family for a long time. Considering this was wartime and the U.S. government had not been very cordial to Japanese-Americans in the past year I couldn't believe what was happening to me.

Alice Richards was the wife of the dean of students at Denison University. One of the traditions the Richards had established was to invite all members of the senior class in small groups for Sunday dinner and an evening of informal conversation with the dean. Margie and I were the only help that Mommie R. had, but she was a good cook and was able to prepare and serve all of the meals. It was an eye-opener for me to observe how the dignified dean and his wife worked together to make these evenings possible and such a popular event. I was impressed even more to observe how she shared in the discussions, assisting her husband in keeping the conversation going on social, political, philosophical and religious issues. That summer I returned to the Rohwer Relocation Center in Arkansas as a social worker. While I was there I received word that Margie, the Richards' daughter, had drowned in Lake Sebago, Maine, where she had gone to be with her fiance and to participate in a Christian student conference. She and another student, who were both excellent swimmers, had gone canoeing and were never to be seen again. Their bodies were never recovered, although the canoe was found.

Margie had been a very popular and active student on campus, and when we returned to school in the fall we all felt the need for a memorial service. The grief the family experienced had to be relived with the many friends who felt the loss and needed comforting. It was Dean and Mrs. Richards who were providing solace to us. As a fairly new person in the Christian faith it was a revelation to me to observe how a devoted Christian family coped with death—especially one as tragic as this one.

The plan was that when I returned from my summer vacation I was to move out of the Richards home and into cooperative housing on campus. I was looking forward to sharing a room with Betty, a student who had spent her summer in an American Friends Service Committee work camp. (These were the days when President Kenneth I. Brown challenged all Denison students to use the summer vacation period in social service.) Betty had been involved in an auto accident in the late summer and had not recovered sufficiently so that she could climb stairs. This meant we could not share our second floor room and she might have to drop out of school for a semester. The Richards came to the rescue and offered their home for Betty's use. Dean Richards would carry Betty up and down the stairs to their second floor bedroom for a number of weeks during her recovery. It was beyond my comprehension how the Richards, who had suffered such a loss, could continue to extend themselves to so many people in so many ways.

It was not too many years later that Dean Richards died, leaving a terrible void for Alice who had now lost the two most important people in her life. Although she had not worked professionally since she married as a junior at Linfield College, Alice was undaunted. The next thing I knew, she was working with Y-teens. It was such a thrill for me to hear her speak out with conviction at the national YWCA convention, publicly taking strong stands on issues I had heard her express in her home during those senior Sunday dinners.

How happy I was the last time I was able to visit her in her home where she served me tea as in the olden days. The memories flowed as we exchanged news of friends, relatives, places, and experiences we had shared in common. At age 91 she was still interested and eager to hear what I was doing and thinking.

The day the letter came asking me to write this article, I received in the same mail the announcement of the death of Alice Louise Wood Richards.

"When she dies, she must shine amongst apostles, and saints and martyrs; she must stand amongst the first servants of God, and be glorious amongst those that have fought the good fight, and finished their course with joy."   (William Law, 1728)

Ms. Tai Shigaki worked for twenty-five years for the Minnesota Department of Corrections until her retirement in July 1987. She earned her Bachelor of Arts degree from Denison University in Granville, Ohio, focusing on sociology, psychology and religion. She earned her Master's degree in Religious Education from Andover Newton Theological School and a Master's degree in Social Work from the University of Minnesota.

Margie Kernicky

by Beth Hassel

❦

Margie, baptized Margaret Mary Kernicky on October 14, 1942, is a woman who is living the gospel and choosing to serve people, so that they might come to know more deeply the unconditional love of God that she has grown to experience. She also is a woman who is physically "disabled" and who does not allow her disability to stand in the way of her ministry.

Her call to ministry began in 1976, when Margie accepted an invitation from her brother, Mike, to go to a meeting to plan a retreat program for physically disabled persons. Until this point Margie had existed in a very safe environment, with her family, in their home in Yeadon, Pennsylvania. As the last of eleven children, she, like many last children, was loved, protected, and sheltered by her many concerned family members. Margie was educated in Catholic elementary and high schools and is now pursuing a university degree, majoring in English and Religious Studies.

Margie was born with cerebral palsy, a condition that affects the entire nervous system, caused by an injury that occurred during birth. She has the severe type of this disability which is characterized by tremors and spasticity that cause her body to be tight and rigid. Because of this she has difficulty communicating both in speech and in writing. However, this has not inhibited her from creatively communicating through the typewriter, and more recently, through the magic of the computer. Not one to allow her verbal problems to be a stumbling block, she continually works on verbal communication and actively encourages others to have her repeat herself until they understand what she is trying to say. Nothing upsets her more than to have the able-bodied nod in agreement when it is clear to her that they have not understood a word that she has said.

Since that day when she heard the call to help with a retreat, Margie has been a woman in the church who has made a difference in the world despite (or possibly because of) being one of the thirty-five million disabled people in the United States. All ministers must minister from their own experience, enlightened by the gospel and the Spirit. Margie is no exception. She has seen the world from a wheelchair and knows the constant frustration of feeling imprisoned by architectural barriers and by her difficulty in communicating her experience, insights, and spirituality. Even with all of the problems of her disability, she was able to answer that call in 1976.

Part of the call was to join Father Shawn Tracy, O.S.A. (Order of St. Augustine), director of Campus Ministry at Villanova University, and a few other people for a Handicapped Encounter Christ (HEC) retreat in New York City. From that experience Margie and Shawn, with the help of about twenty other people, founded the HEC retreat movement in Philadelphia in February 1977. Margie quickly became the coordinator of the program and the editor of Philadelphia HEC's seasonal newsletter, which is printed and also published in cassette form for the visually impaired. In the spring of 1988 Margie was one of the directors of the 43rd Philadelphia HEC retreat, no small accomplishment for Margie Kernicky and for a movement barely eleven years old.

Life is not as simple nor as glamorous as we can sometimes

make it sound. Margie has learned to live and to accept her disability. Each day as the sun rises, she must say yes to the day, yes to the Creator, and yes to a church and to a society that for the most part has discriminated against the disabled. In truth, just to get up means to struggle, to take time and patiently concentrate just to accomplish the daily tasks of survival: personal hygiene, dressing, eating, and getting where you are going on time. Nothing comes easy for a person with cerebral palsy, whose every action takes an incredible amount of time. When such a woman chooses ministry for a lifestyle, and serves hundreds of persons, both physically abled and disabled, she has indeed chosen a unique ministry and is actively seeking a place for her disabled brothers and sisters in our churches.

Margie's experience has also formed her theology. As a young child she clearly remembers when one of her classmates labeled her a "cripple" for the first time. However, that childhood message that she was a cripple did not lessen the power of the supportive message for life that she was given at the time by her faith-filled mother. Margie states, "as far back as I can remember, Mom more than anyone else in my life was an example of a woman with enormous faith. She continuously encouraged me to keep doing the monotonous exercises, always insisting that I had not reached my fullest potential. I now think that Mom was the pioneer of tough love, always affirming along with disciplining me."

Margie still hears patronizing remarks. Many in our world today do not understand a God who permits rejection and alienation, disability and illness. Margie has become accustomed to being stared at with pity; but it still hurts. In fact, most people only see the disability and stereotype her. They conclude that she is retarded and cannot make decisions for herself.

In restaurants, stores, and other public places, as well as in much of the church, people will not address her directly, or if they do, they assume that she must be addressed as a child or as one who is deaf. Part of her ministry has come to be not only with the obviously disabled, but also with those of us who are disabled in other ways and cannot see God's gifts in others who may be different in some way.

This experience of rejection and misunderstanding has influenced her ministry. She has known the depths of depression, confusion, anger, and frustration, and yet through all of these struggles she has consistently stepped out in faith, remained vulnerable, and has taken the risks to confront and educate, the risks to begin a retreat ministry and work through all of the incredible and minute details necessary to plan and execute retreats for the disabled. She has become a leader and a minister, not only for the abled and disabled who make these retreats together (usually a one-to-one ratio), but for Christians at Villanova University, where she lives and works, as well as in the larger community. Her ministry is as much aimed at recruiting and educating the able-bodied for the retreats as it is aimed at serving the disabled. It is no small accomplishment to help those who have never known or communicated with the disabled to discover that they can develop meaningful friendships among disabled folks who are true members of the Body of Christ. Margie helps all of us to truly understand the people that Jesus loved, cared for, challenged, and healed. Margie is a woman who identifies strongly with the many disabled persons in the New Testament stories, especially the woman who was hemorrhaging for twelve years, who Jesus healed because of her faith.

In all of this Margie is no stranger to God; in fact, she is a strong, extroverted, intelligent woman who is very much in touch with God. She continually wants to grow and does this in many ways. She is pursuing a bachelor's degree at Villanova University, where she resides independently in a guest house. She assists at liturgy planning committee meetings, is a member of Scripture reflection groups, and helps to design prayer experiences for the university community. Daily, Margie reads and meditates with the Scriptures. She is able to network the abled and disabled through her seasonal newsletter and is always present at social justice and theology lectures to remain current in her theology. She often assists the internationally known liturgical music group "He Shall Be Peace," by taping performances, selling their albums and tapes, and providing moral support.

Margie is constantly struggling within herself with the facts that her speech is not always understood and everything takes longer to accomplish. As she says, "My day seems to revolve around the clock and this disturbs me. Speech is a basic tool for communication and the fact that I have difficulty in this area often limits my ministry with other persons, very often because of time once again. Very often, too, I give a curt remark or say something funny to offset what is really going on inside."

Margie believes that ministry is the willingness to share one's talents and gifts with others to the best of one's capabilities. In so doing one shares in the building up of the kingdom of God here on earth. Each has something to share, be it a smile, a "good morning" or just a presence with someone. Margie is able to share the fullness of her capabilities because she is empowered to minister by the Word of God. There are many sections of Scripture that speak powerfully to her. In addition to Psalms 23 and 139, the following two passages from the Bible are of special importance:

> "Come to me all you who are weary and find life burdensome, and I will refresh you. Take my yoke upon your shoulders and learn from me, for I am gentle and humble of heart. Your soul will find rest, for my yoke is easy and my burden light" (Matthew 11:28–31, paraphrased).

> Say to those whose hearts are frightened: Be strong, fear not! Here is your God, he comes with vindication; With divine recompense God comes to save you. Then will the eyes of the blind be opened, the ears of the deaf be cleared; Then will the lame leap like a stag, then the tongue of the dumb will sing. Streams will burst forth from the desert, and rivers in the steppe (Isaiah 35:4–6, paraphrased).

The unique ministry of this unique woman has given her a perspective on what Jesus truly meant when he told us that we are all one in him. She has come to define ministry as the celebration of life. Margie believes that if one is a witness to the truth that comes from the manifestation of God through people, the joys of ministry can be a gift for each one. "I wish," Margie said, "that we in the church were at that point in growth where you would not be asking me how I see *women* in ministry. I think that we all, with our various gifts, women and men, disabled and abled, ought to be able to minister in all ways to one another so that together and in everything we might all praise God."

Beth Hassel is a Presentation Sister of Staten Island, New York, and a campus minister at Villanova University, Villanova, Pennsylvania. At the university Beth is a counselor in a residence hall and coordinates programs in ministry, liturgy and social justice for the community. She has earned master's degrees in Religious Education, Community Counseling and Human Relations, and in Library Science and is currently pursuing a Doctor of Ministry degree at Princeton Theological Seminary.

Eliza Jones Hammond

by Diane B. Williams

*F*or forty years, 68-year-old Eliza Jones Hammond has faithfully delivered the Word of God to whomever and wherever God would send her. Licensed for the gospel ministry since 1948 by the Corinthian Baptist Church in Washington, D.C., Sister Hammond clearly serves as a forerunner to the young Baptist women today who dare to push not only for the license to preach, but also for full ordination and unimpeded entrance into the ministerial doorways ordination unlocks.

From childhood young Eliza was in touch with God. The truth is, she cannot remember a time when she was not consciously aware of an inner stirring, early identified as the promptings of the Spirit. Spiritual talk was commonplace in her home in Lancaster, South Carolina, where she was born on December 8, 1919. As is so typically the story for Afro-American families, born into oppression and just a generation removed from slavery, an undying faith in God was always viewed as the bridge that brought them over. So it was in Eliza's family. Her father, Henry, a farmer, suffered the indignities heaped upon Afro-American men of his generation. He also was a class leader and steward in the Methodist church. Her mother, Lula, a midwife, raised eight children (Eliza was number eight) and equipped them with the necessary coping mechanisms and spiritual skills to withstand the wiles of the racism that would be theirs to bear. She also was a Methodist pastor, serving in that capacity for thirteen years at the Mt. Nebo AME (African Methodist Episcopal) Church and the Centennial AME Zion Church. It was this kind of rich spiritual heritage that gave impetus to the rising spirituality that set the child apart almost from the outset of her life.

Formal recognition of Eliza's uniqueness came at age nine when, during a week-long revival at the New Hope AME Zion Church, she came forward of her own volition to give her life to the Lord. As she recalls it she was on the "mourner's bench" along with nine others. She had been sitting there the entire week, caught up, even as a child, in the often spontaneous and always joyful outpouring of the "saints' " love for Jesus. Eliza could contain herself no longer. She vividly remembers being consumed with an effervescent presence and an overwhelming desire to shout her way to the front. In her heart burned a song, "I'm So Glad I Got My Religion in Time." The Spirit of God was finally released from the wellspring of her being. Unbeknownst to her, she was on her way to a lifetime of service to the Lord.

Opportunities for such service came early. Her minister, recognizing the special "anointing" upon the child, began to call upon Eliza to take part, along with other adults, in various aspects of the worship services. Her enormously powerful singing voice, her love of music, and her willingness to sing whenever asked brought her to the fore as a song leader in the church. Perhaps most amazing was her apparent gift of prayer. With regularity she was called upon to pray for the unsaved. It began in the church with full sanctioning by her pastor. Very little time elapsed, however, before neighbors throughout the community were sending for Eliza Jones to come into their homes to pray for the sick. Throughout it all the prophecies came, "Eliza will become a missionary; Eliza will preach," said those in the know.

The call to preach finally came in February 1948. Eliza was twenty-eight years old and had been married for five years to Cleveland Hammond. The couple had moved to Washington, D.C., and had united with the Corinthian Baptist Church. Although others had early recognized the call on her life, it was never obvious to Eliza. For one thing she had always been somewhat sickly and simply lacked the physical strength to endure the rigors of a full ministry.

Thus it was that in the closing months of 1947 Eliza found herself suffering from yet another bout with sickness. For three months she had been confined to a hospital diagnosed by physicians as having tuberculosis. She credits her mother with challenging her to move from a state of helplessness to a position of faith. "If you stop depending solely on these doctors, God will heal you," the Rev. Mrs. Jones said to her daughter. Eliza took her mother's challenge seriously. In stillness and in a state of expectancy, she began to listen for the voice of the Lord. Her healing was dramatic. The doctors, with a battery of X-rays and tests, could find no sign of illness. They, of course, were puzzled beyond belief. They had not heard as Eliza had heard the voice of the Lord declare unto her, "I am the God of Abraham, Isaac, and Jacob, the Creator of all that is. I can heal you, but you have to get up out of your bed and go downstairs." It took a while, but Eliza obeyed. Healing ensued; a clean bill of health was ultimately forthcoming and two months later, Eliza responded yes to the command by God to "go preach." That was forty years ago; other than a cold now and then, she has not been sick since!

As early as 1948 the Corinthian Baptist Church was willing to license a woman to preach. This occurred in a city where even today many churches adamantly refuse to do so. There never was any question as to whether Sister Hammond was worthy of such a sanctioning by the church. Just as in South Carolina, she had worked diligently in her new church home, distinguishing herself as an anointed woman of God. The vote to license was unanimous, and with the full support of her husband, she was on her way.

It soon became evident that revivals would be her hallmark. The demand for Sister Hammond was phenomenal. Her schedule was a rigorous one. Traveling up and down the East Coast and throughout the country, she once preached nonstop for fourteen weeks. It was common for her to have no fewer than sixteen revivals a year, some of which lasted for two or even three weeks. "Folks would line up outside the door of the Solid Rock Baptist Church in Paterson, New Jersey, waiting to enter the prayer line whenever I would minister in revival," recalls Sister Hammond fondly. Yet one of the greatest blessings was that her husband never once opposed her ministry. Cleveland Hammond, until his death, drove his wife wherever she needed to go that her ministry might be fulfilled.

Sister Hammond always had been interested in learning and in furthering her education. Growing up as a farmer's daughter in a segregated South made it difficult to receive a quality education. While white children were able to complete a full nine-month school year, black children were only allowed four months of school per year. Separate and unequal was the rule. It was more important that black children be available for farming and assisting whites with their crops. Sister Hammond remembers picking three hundred pounds of cotton a day.

Despite the racism, Sister Hammond was able to complete the requirements for graduation from the Clinton Junior College in Rock Hill, South Carolina. She was certified to teach up to the sixth grade, but she always wanted more. With nine children to raise and the constant requests for revivals, returning to school seemed nothing more than a distant dream. Finally her youngest had reached junior high school. The older children and her husband all encouraged her, "The time is now, return to school."

In 1974, at the age of 55, Sister Hammond matriculated at the University of the District of Columbia in a special adult education program for those who had been out of school for a while. She graduated in 1979 with a Bachelor of Arts degree in Sociology/Anthropology. The fall of 1979 found her enrolled as a full-time student at the Howard University School of Divinity. Again, she was in her element, performing well as a student and, as was her custom, gaining recognition by the seminary community as an anointed woman of God. The crowning event came in May 1983 when Eliza Jones Hammond, after successfully completing the prescribed course of study, received the Master of Divinity degree. The dean of the Divinity School honored her by selecting her to give the class prayer. Her voice rang out in the chapel on that momentous day with an authority and power that only can come from one who has spent a lifetime walking intimately with the Lord. Her husband cried. Her whole world seemed perfect.

Such joy was to be short-lived, however. Just three days after graduation, Cleveland Hammond became ill. They both had looked forward to spending time together once Sister Hammond had completed her education. He had made so many sacrifices for her to achieve and now she was hoping to devote time to him. It was not to be. Before the month was out, her husband of forty years was dead.

His death was quite a shock. Everything had happened so quickly. It was difficult to imagine life without him. Theirs, however, had been a spiritual union, and the memories of their life together would forever bring her joy. Once again she looked to the source of her strength and positioned herself in the now more-than-familiar faith stance to weather this most painful of storms.

Tragedy certainly has been no stranger to the Hammond family. While still a student in the seminary, Sister Hammond's granddaughter was tragically killed in an automobile accident. Shortly after the death of her husband, a daughter was involved in yet another very serious automobile accident. This same daughter shortly thereafter became stricken with multiple sclerosis. Undaunted, Sister Hammond is firmly convinced that her trials have only made her stronger. Having nowhere else to go but to God in times of crisis has heightened her spiritual sensitivity. Needing to unleash unlimited faith has produced as a by-product a more profoundly dynamic power akin to that which the New Testament says was manifested in the Upper Room on the day of Pentecost. The greatest gift to grow out of trying times is her increased capacity to love. Caring for her daughter has taught her to love everybody's child. Sister Hammond has no regrets with the life that she has lived.

Indeed, she has lived a very full life. Yes, there have been sorrows, but there also have been many joys. She is very proud that all nine of her children were able to go to college. Eight have graduated and several have advanced degrees. They oftentimes accompany her on preaching engagements and provide the music for the service.

One thing still escapes her: she has yet to be ordained. In the years that she has been in ministry, pastors have come and gone at the Corinthian Baptist Church. Each one brings his own perspective to the question of ordination for women. Most have held to the preponderant view among the black Baptist community in Washington, D.C., that women ought not to be ordained.

Opportunities for ordination have come from other denominations and even from other Baptist pastors who recognize God's call in her life and who are willing to take a stand for the cause of women in ministry. Additionally, there are thirteen ministers in her family, one of whom is her brother, pastor of the New Mount Carmel Baptist Church in Washington. Ordination is accessible to her. It is her dream, however, to receive ordination from the church in which she and her family have worshipped and worked throughout her ministry. She loves her church and has received over the years an outpouring of love from the many members of Corinthian. Sister Hammond believes God is able. Ordination is just up the road!

The Reverend Diane B. Williams is the senior pastor of the New Genesis Baptist Church, Washington, D.C. She is a graduate of the University of Maryland and the Howard University School of Divinity and currently is specializing in Urban Ministries in the Doctor of Ministry program at Howard. For the past nine years, she has taught biblical studies in the Continuing Education Department at the Howard School of Divinity. Rev. Williams holds a certificate in pastoral care from the Association of Clinical Pastoral Education for having completed the intern year at Saint Elizabeths Hospital, Washington, D.C. She is a member of the Association of Mental Health Clergy.

Carrie Bell Brown

by Kristy Arnesen Pullen

Carrie Bell Brown is in a very different place now than when she dreamed of being a mortician back in her hometown of Frogmore, S.C. Part of her dream in those days was to compete with the two male funeral directors in town. "I envisioned a funeral parlor painted pink with soft lights," Carrie says. Those dreams were left behind in the eighth grade when she decided she'd "rather work with the living."

Ms. Brown now serves in Ohio as director of the Dayton Christian Center, one of 17 such centers nationwide supported by American Baptists. Her journey in ministry began as a teenager at the Mather School in Beaufort, S.C., during a religious emphasis week. Influenced by the pastor of that week, Dr. Lee Shane, and the week's theme hymn, "Have Thine Own Way, Lord," Brown decided to become a missionary. Friends told her she "had rocks in her head." They thought she should become a teacher, a popular vocation for blacks at that time. That advice helped confirm her decision; Carrie wanted to be different.

Her parents' examples no doubt had something to do with Brown's desire to be her own person. Never aiming at a traditional female role, she takes issue with those who stereotype men and women. "When people say women are more nurturing than men, I have to take exception. My dad was far more nurturing than my mother. He was the one who took care of the stomachaches and fevers." Her mother, on the other hand, was highly respected in their community for her business sense.

Brown's parents were not formally educated and could not afford to offer college as an option for their children. Carrie was not deterred; she earned her way through college by working summers, and she graduated from the Baptist Missionary Training School in Chicago with a bachelor's degree in religious education. As one of ten children, she helped her brothers and sisters see that college was something they could obtain for themselves. Carrie eventually went on to earn a master's degree in guidance and counseling from Bradley University in Peoria, Illinois.

Ordination never has been a priority for Carrie. Although it is something she's thought about off and on throughout her ministry, she fears ordination might make people feel distant from her. Since her first position as a children's worker at Friendship House in Peoria, working at a Christian center has held her interest and commitment. After seven years in Peoria she moved on to direct Emmanuel Christian Center in Brooklyn, New York. She returned to Friendship House to work ten more years before assuming her position at the Dayton Christian Center in 1982.

Brown's responsibilities at the Dayton center include administration, staff supervision, fund raising, public relations and "a little of everything else." The center's activities range from ceramics and karate classes to adult education, "Bible Hour," and providing hot meals for neighborhood children. Carrie hopes that the center at some point will be able to provide a youth employment program and greater support for families with acute problems.

Watching Carrie in action, it's obvious that families in the community already receive vital support. On a busy but ordinary day, Brown was told that a neighborhood boy had broken into the center and ransacked a room of donated clothing. When the boy's mother called in tears, Carrie put aside her earlier frustration and gently comforted the mother. She arranged a time for the boy to clean up the room and scheduled a meeting with his mother to discuss Big Brothers and other community programs that could help the family's situation.

Carrie Bell Brown's approach to ministry, realistic yet hopeful, was evident in her comment at the end of that day: "Well, Carrie Bell, you've had problems galore today . . . but you've had some joy, too."

Kristy Arnesen Pullen currently serves as senior editor for Judson Press. Previously, she was resource editor for the evangelism department of National Ministries, American Baptist Churches, USA. Ms. Pullen graduated from the University of South Carolina with a degree in journalism and earned the Master of Arts in Religion degree from Eastern Baptist Theological Seminary in Philadelphia, Pa.

Marta Ezquilín

by Yamina Apolinaris

*H*er name was Marta Ezquilín, but almost everyone called her Doña Marta as a sign of respect. A few others called her Martita (little Marta). This was actually more fitting since she was less than five feet tall and rarely weighed over 100 pounds. I called her "Abuela" (grandma).

Abuela was the sixth child in a family of eleven children, counting only those who survived birth and early childhood. Born in 1888, she was ten years old when "the Americans came to Puerto Rico" (as she used to say). She remembered life before and after that event which was to bring drastic changes to her life and the life of her people. She loved to tell the stories that reflected those changes. One of her favorite ones had to do with the first time she saw "un americano." A very tall, white soldier wandered by her home near the rain forest. He was sweaty and looked very tired. Her older sister warned her not to go near him because he could harm her. But the man looked friendly, although he was speaking in a language she could not understand. She thought the man was thirsty so she gave him some water and then walked away. Already, Abuela was manifesting what was to be her motto in life, "whatever you may be able to do for a person in need, do it as if you are doing it for the Lord."

At the early age of seventeen she got married and began her own family. Her concern for people and desire for helping others made her the town's favorite midwife. She also worked at a tobacco plantation to help sustain her family of nine daughters and four sons. After all her children had been born, the family moved to the city looking for better work and educational opportunities.

We came into each other's lives when she was 65 years old. I was one among many grandchildren, but circumstances made it possible for us to be together for most of the time until her death at age 90. By the time I was born, my grandmother was already an active member of the First Baptist Church of Río Piedras (the university city). This was the oldest and one of the largest congregations on the island. Coming from a devout Catholic family, she grew up as a very active Catholic woman. The change to Protestantism was drastic for it meant that she had to abandon her family's religion. They believed she had turned away from the correct path to follow evil ways. Large figures of saints had, until that time, occupied a very special place in my grandmother's house—at an altar. Having an altar was a family tradition and so was the evening rosary with the participation of all the members of the family. The morning after my grandmother decided to become Protestant, she removed the statues and altar and substituted family devotions for the rosary. She embraced her new faith with even greater enthusiasm and commitment.

Abuela was a woman whose faith was a living force that permeated all of her life, guided all her decisions and undergirded all her actions. Two of her favorite passages helped me to get a clear sense of her own understanding: "Now faith is the assurance of things hoped for, the conviction of things not seen" (Hebrews 11:1 RSV); "I can do all things in Christ who strengthens me" (Philippians 4:13, paraphrased). Over and over I would hear her repeat this affirmation from the writer of the letter to the Philippians, but it never became a cliché for her.

She was well aware of her limitations. She had a clear understanding of the powers and forces that constrained her life against her own will. She had experienced with many others what it was to see children die and potential be wasted because of the lack of basic resources. But she had accepted Christ and believed in him. For my grandmother, among other things this meant that the impossible could be made possible in those who believed enough to put their faith into action.

Abuela was indeed a woman of faith. She had the assurance of a life that was greater than what she was taught to accept. She believed in life, chose life and worked towards its fulfillment. This is the reason that at age sixty-five, when the doctors told her she could no longer care for children because of a chronic heart condition, she embarked wholeheartedly on the task of raising me, her granddaughter.

Faith is what assured my grandmother that, although she never learned how to read or write, she had been called by God to be a minister—a proclaimer of good news—to minister to those in need. She memorized the Scripture verses that she heard at worship or that were read by her children and grandchildren. She claimed for herself the ministry of visitation. She visited the sick persons in the hospitals, most of the time people she did not know. She visited the prisons and anyone who was in need. Everywhere she stopped to talk to people, pray on their behalf, share words of encouragement, distribute Bibles, New Testaments or any other religious literature and help in whatever way she could.

Here was a woman who had to raise a family under hard economic limitations and yet insisted on sharing her home with the homeless, her food with the hungry, her clothes with the naked. In her house no one was a stranger and everyone was to be treated with respect. Though busy with a large family, she always took time to listen to a neighbor and visit the hospitals and prisons to pray for people and share with them a word of hope.

From childhood, through the life of my grandmother I encountered the force of a faith that believed in life abundantly while at the same time continued to strive for things not yet seen. From my grandmother I learned that faith is also a force that produces change, for her faith was directed toward opening doors of possibilities. Our home became a "house church" where people from the neighborhood would gather on Sunday afternoon and Thursday evening for worship and Bible study. There were many children who continued to grow and develop as leaders. My participation began as a child, first observing my grandmother and her style of ministering to the people in need. Her passion for life, her joy and her commitment were a source of inspiration from my early childhood. She encouraged me and others, allowing us to take part in the services, to lead worship, to utilize our gifts, to plan and participate fully in our gatherings. That house church provided me the opportunity to lead and preach and develop my gifts. Abuela opened my doors and helped me see myself as a full person. She challenged me to overcome the barriers, to have faith, to dare to believe in the God who calls everyone, who equips us with diverse gifts and who transforms our limitations into channels of blessings for others.

My grandmother never talked to me specifically about the pastoral ministry; she gave me the opportunity to experience the "ministry" in a variety of ways. I can still remember the joy in her eyes when I shared with her my decision to enter seminary and prepare for the pastoral ministry. The night I was installed to the pastorate of the First Baptist Church of Bayamón, Puerto Rico, she walked into the sanctuary with obvious pride and a sense of accomplishment. Through her life and ministry she had allowed me to hear the voice of God.

My grandmother's faith sharpened my vision and helped me to value life—my own and that of others—to work and strive for life according to the standards of God's reign (respect, equality, peace, justice, unity, love), to hope and work for things not seen with assurance and conviction. She is no longer physically present, but her life continues to bear fruits in and through those of us who were blessed by her ministry.

The Reverend Yamina Apolinaris is Program Manager for Urban Strategy Development for National Ministries, American Baptist Churches, USA. Prior to her appointment, Ms. Apolinaris served for seven years as pastor of First Baptist Church in Bayamón, Puerto Rico, where she was ordained to the ministry. She became the first woman president of the Baptist Churches of Puerto Rico, serving for two terms. Rev. Apolinaris earned her college degree from the University of Puerto Rico and her Master of Divinity degree from Andover Newton Theological School.

Mary Olson

by Johnnie William Skinner, Sr.

M ary Olson's beginnings were in Wisconsin in the Evangelical Church, a small ethnic-minority group of German immigrants and their children. Worshipers in the Evangelical Church understood well the difficulties of surviving as an ethnic-minority community within the melting pot mentality of American civil religion. For to be German in a country that fought two world wars against Germany was to accept second-class citizenship and deny one's heritage. To be evangelical was to worship in back-street churches in middle America. As in other ethnic-minority religions, the Evangelical Church was the center of one's identity and security. It is no accident that even today Mary's commitment to God is a commitment to strengthening the church.

Mary graduated from the University of Wisconsin in Madison with a major in journalism and mass communications. She was editor of the college newspaper, *The Daily Cardinal,* and passionately believed that her call to the world of communications was a response to the belief that "You shall know the truth and the truth shall make you free." In mid-career when she accepted the call to ordained ministry, she carried with her that same passion for openness, dialogue, and "sifting and winnowing."

Mary married Gerald W. Olson, who became a renowned professor of Soil Resource Development with the Agronomy department at Cornell University (Ithaca, New York) and senior consultant with the Food and Agriculture Organization of the United Nations and the United States Agency for International Development. Dr. Olson had a missionary zeal in his crusade against world hunger and for connecting the study of soils and archeology to solutions to poverty and world hunger. Mary and Gerald had three sons and were married for twenty-five years before his death in October 1987.

While at Cornell, Mary came under the influence of Daniel Berrigan, who very pointedly challenged her to find her place in the "white silent majority." She never forgot his plea: "You, Mary, can speak to them as neither I nor the black people of America can because you are one of them; you speak their language, and they will listen to your words."

Mary took the words of Berrigan seriously and began studies at Colgate Rochester Divinity School/Bexley Hall/Crozer Theological Seminary in Rochester, New York, where she earned the Master of Divinity degree and Doctor of Ministry degree.

Mary responded to the call to ministry and was ordained in the United Methodist Church. She began to fulfill her commitment by serving small churches in upstate New York in an Appalachian environment. Mary has two passionate commitments to her ministry: (1) to serve as a catalyst for the revitalization of the church and (2) to give small churches their rightful place within the body of Christ. In fact, Mary's Doctor of Ministry thesis was "Revitalizing a Denomination the Wesleyan Way." Mary also sees her role as being part of the movement for revitalizing Christianity in America in order to strengthen the spiritual and moral character of the nation. She speaks with intensity of the need for open warfare on the mediocrity that is running rampant within the ranks of professional clergy in this country. She calls the hoped-for outcome "The Demise of Mediocrity". Her own first love is preaching and visioning in the institutional church.

Mary Olson currently serves as assistant professor of ministry and director of the Doctor of Ministry and Continuing Education programs at United Theological Seminary in Dayton, Ohio. Mary brings significant gifts to the United Theological Seminary as a woman directing a D. Min. program that is setting the pace for advanced theological education across the country. She has an opportunity to revolutionize theological education and has a commitment to inclusiveness in the church. She has the gift of bringing people of diverse backgrounds together, yet a deep sensitivity to the differences that people bring to groups. One of Mary's disappointments has been to see racism and sexism in places where one would least expect to find them—in American Christianity. "Theological education must set the standards for a country where excellence is celebrated in many different ways and where mediocrity is rooted out."

Mary has a unique opportunity through a seminary that is in the process of creating a movement in theological education. United Theological Seminary has brought together a cadre of black preachers through the Doctor of Ministry program. Mary facilitates a program that has the potential to bring about tremendous change within her denomination and the Christian church at large.

She brings to the Doctor of Ministry program a new sensitivity and awareness that is needed for renewal and revitalization of the church. She coordinates two special groups—the Proctor Fellows and the Thomas Fellows—and has seen black enrollment in the D.Min. program rise about fifty percent. Dr. Samuel D. Proctor, pastor of the Abyssinian Baptist Church in New York City, leads the Proctor Fellows—a group of black preachers from throughout the United States, prominent women and men through whose ministries the black Christian church continues to be renewed. Bishop James S. Thomas leads the Thomas Fellows—a group of predominantly black United Methodist preachers from the East Ohio area.

The future leaves ample room for new growth and development in advanced theological education. What will become of the new direction being taken at United Theological Seminary through the Doctor of Ministry program under the direction of Mary Olson? Only the Lord knows the boundaries.

The Reverend Johnnie William Skinner, Sr., is a graduate of Nyack College, Nyack, New York, with a B.A. degree in philosophy and a graduate of Union Theological Seminary, New York City, with a Master of Divinity degree. He presently is serving as pastor of the Zion Baptist Church, Dayton, Ohio. Prior to coming to Dayton, Rev. Skinner served as a pastor with Dr. Gardner Taylor of Concord Baptist Church of Christ in Brooklyn, New York. Rev. Skinner presently serves on the Black Church Ministry program faculty at the United Theological Seminary in Dayton where he is pursuing his D. Min. degree. He is chairman of the board and president of JWS Associates, Inc., a ministry of evangelism and discipleship development with an emphasis on social justice issues.

Petra A. Urbina

by Ronald J. Arena

———✵———

W hen the Rev. Petra A. Urbina was called to be the pastor of Primera Iglesia Bautista de Santurce (First Baptist Church of Santurce) in Puerto Rico, another pastor in the region remarked, "So you're the one who's going to bury Primera Iglesia Bautista."

Petra was quick on the return. "No, that's not quite right," she said. "God does not call persons to bring death—either to people or institutions. God calls people to bring life."

Since that exchange less than three years ago, Primera Iglesia Bautista's membership has grown from 109 to 145. Attendance during Sunday morning worship often exceeds 150. Programs and activities are scheduled five nights a week. The church, secure in its own well-being, organized another congregation in nearby Las Lomas to better serve that community.

All of these happenings indeed point to life, not death, and all have taken place under Rev. Urbina's capable leadership. None of this has surprised this feisty pastor. "The possibilities," she says, "are as bright as the promises of God."

That phrase may well serve as the trademark of Petra Urbina. Although she shies away from talking much about it, others credit her with being a role model for other women in Puerto Rico. Fourteen women, four of whom are ordained, now serve in pastoral roles in Puerto Rico, a region of 79 American Baptist churches. In addition, five women from Puerto Rico serve in executive positions within the American Baptist Churches, two in the region and three on the national staff.

Petra's vision for ministry began 37 years ago in Cayey as a "missionary," the term then used in Puerto Rico for director of Christian education. After serving in Christian education in several Baptist churches, Petra came to the Baptist Church of Puerto Nuevo. There she was a partner in ministry with the Reverend Rafael Torres-Escobar. This daring pastor had the vision to open the doors of ordination for women within the Puerto Rico Baptist Churches. On May 26, 1979, Petra A. Urbina became the first woman ordained to the Baptist ministry in Puerto Rico. She then served a church in Adjuntas for five-and-a-half years before accepting the call to Santurce, a community of metropolitan San Juan, in 1985.

Petra does not feel that her ordination in any way invalidates her prior experience in ministry. "I did much pastoring as a Christian education director anyway," she says. "I was never ordained before because the time wasn't right. The soil has to be ready to receive the seed."

Despite her self-assuredness in the pastoral role, Urbina does admit to her shortcomings. When the church expressed interest in her as its pastor, she hesitated and voiced a series of potential pitfalls. The conversation with members of the pulpit committee went something like this:

"Don't you know how old I am?" (56 at the time)

"Oh, yes, more or less."

"You said you want more young people here. Why not call a younger pastor?"

"Oh, we've tried that before."

"I don't like to write, you know. I have a sister in Tampa

(Florida), and I'll make a $30 phone call before I'll write her a letter."

"That's okay. We have a good secretary here."

"But I'm not at all good at administration."

"That doesn't matter. We have a good group of persons here. We'll do what is needed."

As Petra remembers, "They paid no attention to what I said. They called me anyway." And after much thought and prayer, she responded affirmatively, convinced that God's hand had pointed her in a direction.

Now it is evident that Urbina's self-imposed limitations have done little to offset her strengths or halt the momentum of the church's ministry. Her energy belies her age; more young people have become involved in the life of the church; newsletters and other written materials are getting produced; and the administration has been effectively maintained.

More importantly, Primera Iglesia Bautista continues to give witness to Christ's victory of life over death. Thanks to Petra Urbina the church's burial has been postponed indefinitely.

Ronald J. Arena is managing editor of *The American Baptist* magazine of Educational Ministries, American Baptist Churches, USA. Mr. Arena joined the American Baptist Office of Communication in November 1982. He previously worked as a reporter for daily newspapers in Massachusetts and New Jersey. He is a graduate of the University of Massachusetts at Amherst, where he majored in journalism and English. Mr. Arena is a member of the Exton Community Baptist Church in Exton, Pa.

Amy C. Reid

by *Nan M. Brown*

———❧———

During my lifetime, I have met numerous women whom I have admired, who have quietly lived and emulated the words of that self-emptying hymn penned by Adelaide A. Pollard almost a century ago, "Have Thine Own Way." The inspiration for writing this hymn came from the prayer of an elderly woman during a prayer meeting who did not bombard God with repeated requests for blessings or materialism, but simply petitioned God for an understanding of God's will for her life.*

Such a woman is Amy C. Reid, a native of Albemarle County, Virginia, born April 1, 1913. As a child Amy dreamed of becoming a missionary. She had listened attentively to the stories told by her mother of the great work that two missionary women had accomplished teaching children and assisting the needy. Even as

*Kenneth Osbeck, *101 More Hymn Stories* (Michigan: Kregel Publications, 1985), pp. 110 & 111.

early as the age of twelve, God was already at work in Amy's life. God led her, along with the missionaries of the Chatman Grove Baptist Church, as they visited, changed the bedding, and cleaned the homes of the elderly and infirm of the Chatman Grove area. Amy was right there assisting them. Her dreams were being fulfilled.

It was at the Chatman Grove Baptist Church, at the age of nine, that Jesus Christ came into her life, and Amy accepted him as her personal Savior.

Even by the early age of twelve, understanding of the Scriptures was being revealed to Amy by the inspiration of the Holy Spirit. She began to teach adults who were eager to listen and who marveled at the authority with which she taught. They knew this little girl with braided plaits, enthusiastically teaching with her hands swinging and waving and fingers pointing to stress her biblical points, was an extraordinary child. To some persons her expertise in the Bible was frightening and incredible. Even at twelve, Amy knew that God had laid divine hands on her, and that the teaching and preaching of the gospel ministry would be her life's work.

Times were difficult for Amy's family. Money was a scarce commodity. Before she knew what was happening, Amy became a school dropout and a member of the work force. At twenty-one she gave up the little comfort of home, her missionary work at Chatman Grove Baptist Church, and did what so many young black women did in those days. She headed for the bright lights of the big city, New York, where she was planning "to have a good time in the ways of the worldly." Nothing happened the way she had planned.

God, in infinite wisdom, had other plans for Amy's life. When she arrived in New York, the pressure on her mind to be back among the people of God overwhelmed her. She sought a church and joined Walker Memorial Baptist Church on East 132nd Street. There she came to grips with herself, settled down, and met wonderful Christian friends.

Amy soon found a job. Realizing her need for more education, she worked during the days and went to school at night.

The more Amy became engrossed in the work of missions

and the work of the church school, the more evident it became that she must preach. But there was a dichotomy. She felt the urge to preach but Amy, like so many others, did not believe that God called women to the gospel ministry. She admitted herself: "I did not want to preach." Nevertheless, there was a power that resembled a mighty rushing wind that kept pushing her on in the direction of preaching.

That great mystic, poet, philosopher and theologian, the late Dr. Howard Thurman, writes: "In any wilderness [experience] the unsuspecting traveler may come upon the burning bush, and discover that the ground upon which he [she] stands is holy ground . . . Religious experience in its profoundest dimension is the finding of man [woman] by God and the finding of God by man [woman]."* As Dr. Thurman relates, Amy had now come to her burning bush where she met God. She describes the vision: "I was walking down the road and came to a crossroad. I became confused and didn't know which way to go. While standing at this crossroad, God's voice spoke to me saying: 'Go preach my Word.' I heard God's voice several times in my vision. Following this burning bush experience, I had no doubt that preaching the gospel of Jesus Christ was my life's work."

Following this call Amy attended the National Bible Institute in New York. Later she enrolled in the Berea Bible Institute, a three-year theological training school, graduating with honors.

Upon graduation Amy referred to herself as a "bootlegger" of the gospel, since it was almost impossible for a woman to be licensed to preach. Nevertheless, there was a Reverend Harding, pastor of Holy Trinity Baptist Church in Brooklyn, New York, who defied the trends of that day and licensed Mrs. Lillian D. Corbett as assistant pastor of Holy Trinity. Dr. E. W. Wainwright, pastor of Shiloh Baptist Church in Harlem, had also licensed Mrs. Nora L. Thomas. It was through the caring assistance of the Reverend Nora Thomas that Amy finally was licensed to preach.

Rev. Thomas took Amy under her wing and accompanied her

*Howard Thurman, *The Creative Encounter* (Indiana: Friends United Press, 1972 and Harper and Row, 1954, pp. 33 & 39.

to talk with her pastor, the Reverend Dr. James W. Tate, about licensing. During the lengthy meeting Amy's pastor agreed that he would permit her to have "missionary papers," but not a license to preach. Amy held to her guns. She knew she had been called to preach and refused to accept the missionary papers.

Amy was determined not to give up, nor to change her Baptist denomination as so many of the Baptist women did during that time. They went on to denominations that would license them to preach.

Finally, Pastor Tate, who had pastored Walker Memorial Baptist Church for forty years and had never licensed a woman to preach before, could see that Amy was determined to follow through on her call. He agreed to have the congregation vote on whether or not Amy could be licensed. The congregation was unanimous in its consent for Amy to preach her first sermon. On July 14, 1942, this determined yet humble saint of God delivered her initial sermon entitled: "Awake and See the Time." With little fanfare she received her license to the gospel ministry. The Reverend Amy C. Reid relates: "It was truly a great feeling. I could go home in the summertime a licensed Baptist preacher."

Rev. Reid had now passed the first test, but what about ordination? Male pastors were not inclined to ordain women in ministry, but does not God have the last word?

A group of women in ministry, some of whom had been ordained in other denominations, organized The Women's Interdenominational Ministerial Conference of America, Inc., in order that those women ministers whose home churches refused to ordain them could be ordained by the conference. Rev. Reid refers to these women as "powerful souls." She recalls, "On the 26th day of June 1944, they laid hands on me. I was ordained to make full proof of the gospel ministry. Most of the women had a hard time making it up [the ladder of success]. Some of the male ministers labeled all women preachers as 'bulldaggers' [lesbians]. None of these things moved me because I knew God had called me and was for me."

In 1947, Amy Reid left the bright lights of New York and returned to her home in Eastham, Virginia, four miles outside of Charlottesville. She went back to worship at the Chatman Grove Baptist Church where Dr. E. D. McCreary, Sr., who did not recognize women preachers, was pastor. In spite of this stance, he finally granted Amy an opportunity to preach and was stunned that she could appropriately prepare and dynamically deliver a sermon.

It is amazing how God always provides someone to help those called to do God's work. Such was the case with Rev. Reid. The Reverend J. B. Johnson, who had returned to Virginia after having spent many years in Maryland, was moderator of an organization called "The Christian Spiritual Union." The purpose of the union was to assist churches financially. Crowds of people attended this union since it was composed of churches in four counties. Then, too, people came to hear the two sermons that were preached, and for the food and fellowship. Rev. Johnson gave Amy Reid a chance of a lifetime—an opportunity to preach one of the sermons. Rev. Reid preached out of the depths of her heart.

The Christian Spiritual Union became the springboard for her ministry. Rev. Reid relates: "I was the only woman preacher, Baptist or otherwise. These local people had never heard a woman preach. Everyone was anxious to meet and hear me. So, from that time on, I never lacked an opportunity to preach. Doors opened for me to preach everywhere—in town as well as in rural areas. Most of the male ministers who did not accept or believe in me were forced to give me a chance. Their congregations demanded to hear me. Once these men heard me they confessed that they never would say again that God did not call a woman to preach."

In Rev. Reid's forty-five years of preaching the gospel, she has preached for revivals, during absences of ministers from their pulpits, and for special occasions. She has never had to ask anyone for an opportunity to preach. God has always made a way.

In 1949, Rev. Reid, working together with a great Christian missionary and later preacher, Mrs. Phrindessia Chew, sponsored classes in Bible teaching and preaching at a church in

Northern Albemarle County in the rural mountains of Gordons-ville, Virginia. The church had been closed for years but was in an area where there was a great evangelistic need. Following Rev. Reid's preaching and Mrs. Chew's prayers on that Sunday in October 1949, Rev. Reid was asked to return and preach again. During this second preaching visit, Rev. Reid was asked to reopen the Wildon Grove Baptist Church and become its pastor. She accepted this call, reorganized the church and has served the church with distinction for the past thirty-eight years. She states: "Many souls came to the Lord as a result of the work there." In 1972, a new edifice was built.

In 1977, Rev. Reid was asked to serve for one year as acting pastor of the Pleasant Grove Baptist Church, Earlysville, Vir-ginia. After having served for only a few months, she was called to be the regular pastor of this barely surviving church. During her pastorate there has been a great deal of progress made, numerically and spiritually, and the church building has been renovated. Rev. Reid is always busy at both Wildon Grove and Pleasant Grove, active in Church Women United, The Lott Carey Convention, and is untiringly giving her efforts to foreign missions.

Reverend Reid in her kind, sweet way adds: "It is my belief that God gives to each servant a special work to do in special places. I pray that when my life is ended, I will have fulfilled that place and completed the work that the Lord has assigned to my heart and hands to do."

The Reverend Nan M. Brown had served with distinction as senior pastor of the Mount Level Baptist Church, Dinwiddie, Vir-ginia, when she became the first woman graduate of the Virginia University School of Theology to pastor a black Baptist church. She is currently senior pastor of the New Hope Baptist Church, Esmont, Virginia. Ms. Brown received the Bachelor of Science degree from the District of Columbia Teachers College, Washington, D.C., and the Master of Divinity degree, magna cum laude, from the Virginia Union University School of Theology, Richmond, Virginia. Prior to her second career as a pastor, she was employed by the U.S. Government for more than twenty-eight years and retired in 1976 as national director of the Federal Women's Program, U. S. Department of the Interior, Washington, D. C. She is an author, whose first book, *The Patience To Wait,* has just been published.

Emily Gibbes

by Preston Robert Washington

—✵—

Emily Gibbes, one who exemplifies what the biblical writers refer to as "whatsoever is lovely," is commonly referred to as the "mother of inclusive language." In her pioneering and visionary role in Christian education, she prodded and pushed for more than seven years for the development of an inclusive language lectionary, which has affected the life of more than thirty-two denominations. Active in Christian life for more than 70 years, she has helped to mold and shape the lives of many church leaders, past and present. Even today after twice retiring she continues to serve with vigor, provoking much thought at the New York Theological Seminary (NYTS). She has been at NYTS since 1981, developing the Religious Education program for the seminary and serving as mentor for the Doctor of Ministry program.

But her Christian journey, which dates back to her childhood, had more meager beginnings. Emily was born in 1915 in the

Harlem section of New York, a neighborhood known as "Strivers' Row" where many of the black professional and middle class resided. Her father, although not an active church-goer, was a general practitioner of medicine for 37 years, and the son of an AME (African Methodist Episcopal) preacher. Her mother was actively involved in the Salem United Methodist Church, where Emily received her earliest Christian education.

At about the age of ten, she began attending the St. James Presbyterian Church, also in Harlem, under the leadership of Dr. William Lloyd Imes. Both he and his wife played a significant and positive role in Emily's life and future. Dr. Imes' moving sermons began to "stir something within"—sermons that talked about the need for inner strength, self-criticism and self examination, particularly for black people. It was this church family that ultimately showed Emily the nurturing role of the church. It created an atmosphere that exuded the message: "We love kids; we celebrate the presence of young people." This was demonstrated by the fact that although St. James had no paid Sunday school staff they provided one of the most excellent church schools in New York City, with sixty staff volunteers, 600 students and five children's choirs. Emily's relationship with St. James allowed her leadership gifts to be discovered and used. She became very involved, from being one of the children sent away to camp each summer, on through college, when she continued teaching in the church's ministry and became superintendent of the Junior Department of the church school. She later became superintendent of the entire church school.

Emily's formal education included a Bachelor of Arts degree from Fordham University in N.Y. Later in 1952, as she listened to the call in her life to become proficient in Christian education, she earned a Master of Religious Education degree from New York University.

Her life, which spans over three-quarters of a century, has been woven like the richly colored threads of the African *Kente* cloth. This woman from Harlem's Strivers' Row ultimately became an international ambassador of goodwill, a leader in the church world, a reconciler, a pioneer and a healer. As men and women watch her movement, they describe her as one who moves with graciousness, poise and beauty, making her an important woman who brought her gifts to Jesus, to be used for his glory.

Even at a time where there were very few role models for women to emulate in professional church work, Emily developed a relationship with Dorothy Height, now the head of the National Council of Negro Women, who presented Emily with the life-transforming idea that she could become a paid worker for the church. Emily then worked for many years in the New York City (N.Y.C.) Mission Society's Camp Minisink, while also taking courses at Union Theological Seminary.

For a time Emily found herself in a political arena although she says she is not "political." She became administrative secretary to Mrs. Genevieve B. Earle, a white woman and the first female member of the N.Y.C. Council. Twice Emily successfully managed Mrs. Earle's campaign, helping her to win. After six years in this explosive political arena, Emily returned to mission and nurture in the church.

She then became secretary of the Board of Christian Education for the National Presbyterian Church and was the first black person to work in the entire building of that national office. Eventually, with some personal and financial sacrifice, Emily became the first black and the first female Christian education field representative, serving 166 Presbyterian churches from northern Westchester County to Montauk Point, Long Island.

Her reputation began to spread throughout the nation for the magnificent job that she was doing in a variety of executive capacities. In 1954, she became the first black on the national staff of the Presbyterian Church. She eventually went overseas and worked in French Cameroon as a consultant in religious education and then taught in Kenya. It was these and other experiences in Africa that Emily describes as a wonderful experience . . . allowing her the opportunity to come to know the indigenous Christian persons on the African continent, who she says, "have so much to teach *us,* given the limitations of our Western missionary understanding."

As part of a team of women, she spent eight months in India, meeting with women from across India and Pakistan, opening the door for goodwill among the females of these nations and advancing reconciliation and interracial/intercultural understanding. Her travel became more extensive and later included countries such as Japan, Hong Kong and Thailand.

Longing to continue learning, she returned to the States and became associate general secretary for the National Council of the Churches of Christ's Division of Education and Ministry and then accepted a position with Friendship Press. She also encountered what she describes as one of the most incredible growing edges of her life, her so-called retirement. In 1980, she went to Puerto Rico to become acclimated to the Hispanic community, since she had gotten to know many Hispanic people at the New York Theological Seminary. It also was at N.Y.T.S. that she saw a tremendous burden and commitment to ministry in the urban metropolis.

Emily was never ordained, but in retrospect would do so if she had life to live over again. But, she paved the way for women and men who wanted vocations as workers in the church. Emily has a strong desire for young people to take advantage of life's opportunities. She is reminded of her own home where the message as a child was clearly expressed, "You can get anything you want if you prepare yourself." It remains to be seen whether or not Emily has gotten everything she desired in life, but the span of her life and great accomplishments indicate that she has given back to God the best that she has.

Who would have thought that a little black girl from Harlem would do so much for inclusive language, and for both men and women in ministry. At times risking job and reputation, through many tear-filled years, she has helped to open up the Scriptures in new ways for all of God's children and continues to do so today.

The Reverend Preston Robert Washington has been the pastor of Memorial Baptist Church in Harlem since 1976. Dr. Washington earned his Bachelor of Arts degree from Williams College in Massachusetts, the Master of Divinity degree from Union Theological

Seminary in New York, and recently earned the Doctor of Education degree at Columbia University. He is professor of Religious Education at New York Theological Seminary and the author of the recently released Judson Press book, *God's Transforming Spirit: Black Church Renewal.*